got debt?

THE **7 BULLETPROOF STEPS** TO DEBT FREEDOM

How we paid off $100,000 in 12 months

Leo Jean-Louis

The topics of finance and debt are serious matters with real-life consequences. This book was written to share the steps that enabled my wife and I to be successful on our journey to debt freedom. We wholeheartedly believe this book will educate and empower you to overcome your debt. However, I am not a financial professional. Before taking any of the actions recommended herein, please seek the counsel of a financial advisor/planner, attorney, accountant, or other tax professional.

DEDICATION

To my wife, Faith; my helpmate, the keeper of our home and absolute Wonder Woman. Thank you for believing in the vision God gave me for our family. You jumped right in and put your hands to the plow, you sacrificed greatly, and endured this journey to freedom with so much grace. Those on the outside will never be able to fully see how integral you were in this process, but I have, and there is no way we would have made it this far without you. For that, I am forever grateful. May the legacy we leave behind be proof that the choices we made were all worth it.

To my unborn baby; your impact is already felt and everything we have done was to prepare for your arrival. Let our home be the place where your voice is heard, and your dreams are allowed to flourish. May the yes's and no's you receive from us be based on our decisions to parent you best and not out of fear from financial pressure or limitations. More importantly, may you grow to know and love God and walk confidently in the purpose He has already established for you.

To my mother; I know it was no small sacrifice for you

to watch your only child grow up from afar, however, you knew America would offer me far more opportunity than your motherland. Your fervent prayers have sustained me, and your unwavering work ethic has been a blueprint on my financial journey. Despite the distance, we have been closer than one would think as your unconditional love always prevailed. For all these things and so much more, I thank you.

FREEDOM
free·dom
/ˈfrēdəm/
noun

Freedom
The state of being free or at liberty rather than in confinement.
Exemption from external control, interference, or regulation.
The power to determine action without restraint.
Freedom
What most desire but never achieve.
It screams loudly to those whose ears are sensitive enough to hear, compelling them to action for a worthy cause.
To them, freedom is not an illusion. It's a lifestyle worth fighting for.
Freedom… is a choice!

CONTENTS

ACKNOWLEDGMENTS

To all of you in the debt-free community who have supported *Freedom Is A Choice Movement*, thank you! Your kind words and well wishes have been greatly appreciated. Your enthusiasm to pursue debt freedom has been refreshing and encouraging; I am excited to see generations changed because you decided to take control of your finances and get out of debt. Freedom is a choice and I'm so glad you have chosen freedom!

FOREWORD

LEO JEAN-LOUIS IS ONE OF THE HARDEST working men I know. He's consistent, loyal and determined. These characteristics have helped him and his wife, Faith, eliminate over $100,000 of debt. Their journey to debt freedom has been inspirational, edifying and uplifting.

I have known Leo for many years, and I've had the honor of pastoring him, officiating his wedding and encouraging him to get serious about eliminating debt. During one of his premarital advisement sessions, we spoke about their debt, and they decided to eliminate it once and for all. Their unwillingness to compromise and maintain their resolve is impressive and worth emulating.

Leo has been a permanent fixture in our community of believers. His service and dedication have won him the respect of his peers. I have been impressed with him from the day I met him, and I am honored to have known him for many years. What impresses me most about him is his willingness to leave his family a legacy of freedom, discipline and hard work. His decision to lead his family to eliminate debt will affect every generation to come long after him. He is charting a new course for his family, and his children's children will appreciate him for it.

What's even more impressive is that he is willing to

share his wisdom with you in this book. I would recommend that you do not see this as another get out of debt book but as an opportunity to chart a new course for your family and build a legacy for generations to come. Throughout the book you will learn how to get out of debt, but most importantly, you will discover a stronger you. You will discover the *why* behind the *what* to propel you to finally let go of the burden that has held you and your family down for years, if not decades.

I not only recommend Leo as an author, but I recommend him as a person. Prepare to be challenged, encouraged and uplifted as you journey through the wisdom of a gifted and disciplined man. I pray that you are challenged by what's written herein and resolve to eliminate the burden of debt once and for all.

May God bless you.

Cornelius Lindsey

INTRODUCTION

T HE WAR AGAINST DEBT IS A TWO-PART ISSUE - the battle against ourselves and the battle against the lending institutions.

Chapter 1

CONTACT LEFT, 9 O'CLOCK…
MULTIPLE SUSPECTS

Under Siege

A siege is defined as the act or process of <u>surrounding and attacking</u> a fortified place in such a way as to isolate it from help and supplies, <u>for the purpose of lessening the resistance</u> of the defenders and thereby <u>making capture possible</u>.

EIGHTY PERCENT OF AMERICANS ARE IN DEBT. That means 8 out of the next 10 people you meet are in the red. Seventy-three percent of them will take their debt with them to the grave.[1] That is no way to live. How are Americans really living?

Take a look at some of these alarming study highlights from a recent survey conducted online by Harris Poll on behalf of CareerBuilder from May 24 to June 16, 2017.[2]

- 78 percent of U.S. workers live paycheck to paycheck to make ends meet.

- Nearly 1 in 10 workers making $100,000+ live paycheck to paycheck.
- More than 1 in 4 workers do not set aside any savings each month.
- Nearly 3 in 4 workers say they are in debt today - more than half think they will always be.

Furthermore, according to the Federal Reserve's "Report on the Economic Well-Being of U.S. Households in 2017," over one-fifth of adults are not able to pay all of their current month's bills in full.[3] The term that has been coined for millions of Americans who find themselves in such dire circumstances is *financially fragile*, meaning they are often one misfortune away from complete ruin. These individuals can barely save enough money for an emergency.

There are two ways to conquer and enslave a nation. One is by the sword, the other is by debt. - Anonymous

A big reason behind these statistics is the four-letter word called debt. Americans are borrowing money more than ever and banks are lending people money they cannot afford to pay back. This is most evident in the case of the student debt crisis where it is not uncommon to hear stories of student borrowers owing massive amounts of debt as the price of college tuition increases almost eight times faster than wages.[4] Student debt is a

$140 billion a year industry. While students are struggling to pay off their debt, the government and private companies are continuing to thrive from this goldmine. Of course, some of the onus is on the borrower who willingly took out loans they could not afford. However, more often than not, the criticism is directed toward the borrower while the involvement of the lending institutions is neglected. One can argue that responsibility is not solely required on the part of the borrower. Ownership also needs to be taken by the lending institutions who deliberately give out these loans for what seems to be driven by this one frank reality – those who are unable to pay back their debt (or unable to pay it back in a timely manner) are much more profitable than those who are able to stay on top of it. Below is a statement from Sen. Elizabeth Warren (D-Mass) regarding the student debt crisis:

> *The United States government turns young people who are trying to get an education into profit centers to bring in more revenue for the federal government. This is obscene. The federal government should be helping students get an education – not making a profit off their backs.*[5]

If you want to find someone who has made a handsome profit from the backs of student loans, look no further than the CEO of everyone's favorite student loan service provider - Sallie Mae. Albert Lord's (CEO of Sallie

Mae) *compensation topped $200 million* from 1999-2004. From 2010 to 2013, when students began to take on more debt, Sallie Mae's profits were a whopping $3.5 billion! Before retiring in 2013, Lord became one of the highest paid executives in Washington and even built his own private golf course![5]

However, student loan debt is not the only area where individuals become easy targets of lending institutions. Here is an interview I conducted with the Owner Loyalty Manager/Customer Relations Manager at a local Nissan dealership recently.

Me: What tactics are used in your industry to drive sales?

Manager: So when it comes to tactics, I wouldn't say there are set tactics we use. We more so approach it with the mindset of which method of sale will bring the most money. And to the dealership world, that means *financing.* All vehicle dealerships purchase the vehicle from the manufacturer at a low price as franchise partners. So, when purchasing/leasing we really have room to *make a profit* on both the front end (car purchase) and the back end (financing/warranties). This is especially true when it comes to leasing.

Me: How do you determine what a good profit is?

Manager: We are paid as a dealer in finance by a point system based on the consumer's buy rate. So, the *goal* is the *higher the buy rate,* the *fatter the pocket.* Locking the consumer into a higher buy rate means payment is usually higher on a shorter-term loan. But what we do is offer a longer loan term as an option to the consumer. This translates into a more affordable payment and a higher likelihood we will close the deal. The result of a longer term is *more money to us in the form of interest.*

Me: Tell me more about how you make profit on the back end?

Manager: We make money on the back end as well when selling warranties. The manufacturer trusts the products they build and study how often major malfunctions occur in their vehicles. It's not very often. Consumers almost never get the full use of their warranties. But our goal is to sell the extended warranty!

Me: That's interesting!

Manager: Same with leasing but we like leasing more. With leasing, we know the vehicle is set to depreciate. We basically calculate how much it will lose in value for the term of the lease (considering it's not damaged) and charge you that amount and then some as profit. We also get you with mileage fees if you go over and with your inspection once you turn in your vehicle. Hopefully, we got a few warranty contracts out of you too!

Perhaps the most telling story is the recent scandal by Wells Fargo, whose employees secretly opened over 3.5 million fraudulent bank accounts and credit cards all in the names of their existing customers without their knowledge or consent.[6] Regulators say funds were removed from customer's existing accounts and transferred into newly created ones. Some workers altered documents about business customers, amongst several other illegal practices. It's reported that these egregious and illegal acts occurred between 2011 to 2015. Not only did these fake accounts earn Wells Fargo hundreds of thousands of dollars in the form of interest charges, unwarranted fees, and overdraft protection fees, it allowed employees to boost their sales figures to earn bonuses. Customers were being charged for accounts they did not even know existed and some of those accounts were sent to collections. Here's a shocking list revealing more of what federal regulators, including the Consumer Financial Protection Bureau (CFPB), found during their investigation.[7]

- Wells Fargo admitted they charged at least 570,000 customers car insurance they did not need. Some 20,000 customers defaulted on their loans for related reasons and eventually had their vehicles repossessed as a result.

- Wells Fargo charged their customers for pet insurance and other products that were not fully understood.

Now, this is not to say that all banks or lending institutions act unethically. I mention this only to provide insight into the framework by which some lending institutions operate. In the case of Wells Fargo, their unrealistic incentive compensation plans and high-pressure sales culture drove the inappropriate behavior that led to these events. So, it is not farfetched to presume this type of culture exists to some extent today at other lending institutions. The sales pressure often placed on employees to reach unattainable quotas leaves me questioning the intentions of such institutions. Do they exist to genuinely help the customer or prey upon them?

Because of debt, people are putting off major life goals such as retirement, buying a home, getting married, and having children. We are under siege. While increasing our awareness of what the lending institutions are doing is one step toward solving the problem, the other step is addressing the battle within. While I am aware some individuals are in debt due to circumstances beyond their control, many of us are in debt because of a *series of choices* we made along the way. Did you know that freedom is also a choice? I want you to choose freedom today. This book will equip you with the 7 Bulletproof Steps you need to win the war against both.

MY HOPE

If you are reading this book, then you are either in debt yourself or know someone who is. This book is written for those who find themselves in that predicament. It is written for the new college graduate who is drowning in thousands of dollars of debt before ever earning his/her first career paycheck. It is written for the 45-year-old man or woman who has spent the last 20 years making minimum payments and never seeming to get ahead in life. It is written for everyone in between, who deep down know their debt is an issue that needs to be addressed but struggle to get started or simply don't know how. My goal is to equip you with a proven step-by-step guide you can easily follow and implement. My desire is to inspire everyone, everywhere, to strip off the weight of debt that slows them down and inevitably prevents them from living out their God-given purpose. My hope is that you would believe freedom from debt is possible, and to choose for yourself, a life of freedom.

Critical Thinking Questions

1. The title of the chapter *Contact left, 9 o'clock… Multiple Suspects* is derived from code words used in war to describe where shots from the enemy are being fired from. These code words are used to notify troops where to look and from which direction to be on guard. *Contact left* signifies shots are being fired from the west (the left side). "*9 o'clock* signifies the approximate location, as in where the 9 is on a standard clock. *Multiple suspects* indicate that shots are being fired by multiple people.

   Regarding finances, what are some ways we, as a society, are *under siege* (aka under attack) by the lending institutions?

2. While the lending institutions are a clear enemy, do you think we can be our own enemies in terms of our personal choices, our mindset, or our habits? If so, in what ways?

Chapter 2

BORROW, LEST YOU BE FREE
Booby Trap

Punji sticks, snake pits, the mace, and flag bombs were some of the most terrifying Vietnam War booby traps. As bait, they <u>lured</u> unsuspecting soldiers <u>toward</u> severe <u>physical injury</u> or their <u>demise</u>. Their impact on the War was profound, rendering the more powerful and better trained U.S. military less effective in their pursuit.

ON MAY 23, 2018, my wife, Faith, and I paid off a total of $104,221.89 of debt in 12 months! Yes, 12 months! How exactly did we do it? I knew you would ask! I also know you would cringe if I told you that by the age of 26 and 29, respectively, our combined debt once we said "I do" was over $211,000! Why did we allow ourselves to accumulate so much debt to begin with? We'll get to that part later. Let us first recount the recent history of debt in America.

The United States' national debt, exceeding $21 trillion, is the highest for a single country in the world. To put this into perspective, the U.S. national debt is only slightly higher than that of the European Union, an economic union comprised of 28 countries. The debt-to-gross domestic product (GDP) ratio is a tool used by economists and investors to compare what a country owes and what it produces. A low debt-to-GDP ratio indicates a country can pay back its debt without having to incur further debt; this is possible because the country produces and/or sells enough goods and services. On the contrary, a high debt-to-GDP ratio indicates a country is not producing and/or selling enough to pay back its debt; this consequently leads to a higher risk of default and the propensity to incur further debt. Currently, the U.S. debt-to-GDP ratio is an astonishing 105.40%![1] At this rate, America is borrowing more than the economy can generate in revenue. Will America ever pay its debt back? Does this at all sound familiar to your current situation involving debt?

While the national debt reveals the government's spending habits, statistics show the apple doesn't fall far from the tree when exploring the spending habits of the US household. According to the "Quarterly Report on Household Debt and Credit" published by the Federal Reserve Bank of New York's Center for Microeconomic Data, household debt soared to a record-breaking $13.51 trillion in the third quarter of 2018. Mortgage debt rose by $141 billion to $9.14 trillion; student loan debt accounted for $1.44 trillion. Auto loans continued to trend upward to $1.27 trillion, while credit card debt rose by $15 billion to $844 billion.[2]

Household Debt and Credit Developments as of Q3 2018[2]

CATEGORY	QUARTERLY CHANGE*	ANNUAL CHANGE** (BILLIONS $)	TOTAL AS OF Q3 2018 (TRILLIONS $)
MORTGAGE	(+) $141 BILLION	(+) $397	$9.140 TRILLION
HOME EQUITY LINE OF CREDIT	(-) $10 BILLION	(-) $26	$0.422 TRILLION
STUDENT LOAN	(+) $37 BILLION	(+) $85	$1.442 TRILLION
AUTO LOAN	(+) $27 BILLION	(+) $52	$1.265 TRILLION
CREDIT CARD	(+) $15 BILLION	(+) $36	$844 BILLION
TOTAL DEBT	**(+) $219 BILLION**	**(+) $557**	**$13.512 TRILLION**

*Change from Q2 2018 to Q2 2018   **Change from Q3 2017 to Q3 2018
Table 1. Retrieved from
https://www.newyorkfed.org/newsevents/news/research/2018/rp181116

Consider this reality. Most people are in debt as soon as they enter the "real world" and most people remain in debt until they die. The pattern modeled for us is to borrow money for everything we desire even if our accounts or savings don't support it. We are trained to borrow money to pay for college, to buy a car, to buy a house, and the list goes on. The availability and misuse of credit cards has further exacerbated the problem by placing large sums of money at our fingertips. We swipe on impulse as we succumb to the overstimulation of marketing and advertising techniques strategically placed in buildings, on buses, billboards, radio, television, and social media. The majority of Americans live paycheck to paycheck and believe they could not survive without debt. These are the same individuals who are not able to save enough for an emergency, who worry about not having enough for retirement, and are overwhelmed by the constant stress produced by trying to live a lifestyle they cannot sustain. What was supposedly designed to help us has instead enslaved us. Slavery, as we know it, kept people oppressed and I would argue that debt does the exact same.

How America's debt became so large is beyond the scope of this book. However, I did not forget your question from earlier. How did my wife and I allow ourselves to accumulate so much debt to begin with? The answer, quite frankly, is that we did not know any better. We thought applying for loans was the only way we could obtain the funds needed to pursue our goals. Could it be that the same sentiment the government seems to have toward its debt has somehow infiltrated the perspectives we as a society have on accumulating debt? Does that same sentiment lead to widespread apathy amongst the population, resulting in no desire to ever pay back their debt?

A Walk Down Memory Lane

I recall the day I received my acceptance letter to the University of Massachusetts Amherst (UMass)! I had absolutely no idea what field of study I was going to pursue, but boy was I overjoyed at the thought of leaving home and living independently on campus for the next four years of my life. The summer prior to my first semester in college was largely spent buying school supplies, shopping for items for my dorm room, packing suitcases, and spending time with friends reminiscing on the good ol' days. I stepped out of the navy-blue Dodge minivan my uncle had driven my cousin and I in, adjacent to the Coolidge Tower dorm rooms on the southwest side of campus. Immediately, I was greeted by the smell of freshly cut grass on a hot summer day, the sound of suitcases being rolled in multiple directions on the concrete as cars were being unloaded, and the long line of freshmen standing with their parents, anxiously waiting to be checked in. "Welcome to freedom," I thought to myself. Wrong. During all the preparation and paperwork that went into applying for and finally attending college, I would later discover I had signed myself into slavery.

Twelve years removed from my first experience on a college campus, I vaguely remember having any in depth conversations regarding the cost to attend college and how to pay for it. While high school prepared us for the SATs and encouraged us to get the GPA needed to be accepted into college, there was little to no education on financial literacy, entrepreneurialism, or acquiring skill sets that allow you to make a decent living without a college degree, such as tech jobs, plumbing, electrical, etc. While our parents spoke to us constantly about behaving ourselves and encouraged us to focus on our studies, there was little to no education on budgeting, the benefits of first attending a community college to satisfy general education requirements, or the ramifications of borrowing money. It seemed like the only option presented to us after high school was to go to college. It was the thing to do! Those who did not were frowned upon by many. The hidden reality was that once we graduated and started our careers, the subsequent years of our lives would be spent digging ourselves out of debt, well for most of us, digging ourselves further into debt.

"I'm never going to pay my debt off," some would say. Wrong, again. Included in the many documents you were required to sign during the Free Application for Federal Student Aid (FAFSA) process, was a legal document titled *promissory note*. The Oxford Dictionary defines a promissory note as a signed document containing a written promise to pay a stated sum to a specified person or the bearer at a specified date or on demand. Do you recall signing this document? I vaguely remember and can assuredly tell you I did not take the time to adequately consider the implications of borrowing money. Unsurprisingly, the promissory note is not limited to the FAFSA process. In fact, institutions such as auto dealerships and banks who finance auto, mortgage, and personal loans have their own version of a promissory note (i.e. financing agreement or contract) that is required to be signed. And the moment you signed that document, you surrendered your right to be free. Remember what the promissory note is? It is the *promise* you made to *pay back* a stated sum at a specific time. Have you ever let someone borrow something? Did you expect it back? And in a reasonable amount of time? We believe it is your responsibility to pay back your debt. It is a question of character to not keep your word. Furthermore, it is a question of integrity to have no intent or plan in place to repay what you knowingly *borrowed*.

The Breakdown of Our Debt

Type of Debt	Amount Owed	Lending Institution
Credit Cards	$9,400	Bank of America
Student Loans	~$197,000	Fed Loan, Sallie Mae, Great Lakes, Discover, Heartland
HVAC Loan	$5,386	Wells Fargo

Table 2.

The borrower is slave to the lender.
- Proverbs 22:7 NIV

When I graduated from my Master's program in 2013, the last thing on my mind was paying back my student loans. I had just sacrificed the last 4-6 years of my life (between college and graduate school) living below my means and I was finally ready to start enjoying the fruit of my labor. I was pleased to hear I would be given a six-month grace period for my federal student loans but, like most, I thought the time frame was too short. The six months was a blur. It took me a few months to pass my boards and become licensed and another two months to land my first career job. With one month remaining until my grace period ended, I was in no shape to start making payments toward my loans. I panicked and called my federal student loan service provider. They presented me with several repayment options, and of course, any payment was too much in my estimation. After the representative exhausted all repayment options with me, she informed me of the hidden treasure – forbearance. "Now that's more like it," I thought to myself. Forbearance is a period during which you can temporarily stop making student loan payments under certain circumstances, such as hardship. Well, to me, anything at that time preventing me from being able to spend as I pleased was a hardship. I signed up immediately! Little did I know, it would come back to haunt me.

Debt Can Affect Your Ability to Buy A Home

Two years into my career, I decided it was time to purchase my first home. The cost to rent my 796 sq. ft. 1-

bedroom apartment in Atlanta was increasing, yet again, but now to $1,100/month, and I knew I could not continue to throw money down the drain by funding someone else's retirement account. I contacted a local real estate agent who walked me through the home buying process. Per her direction, I then reached out to a mortgage lender and spoke to a loan officer who informed me of the amount of *house* I qualified for; the amount I was approved for was of course way more than what I needed. At the time, Faith and I were courting, so she went along with me to the open houses. Among the homes we viewed, one in particular, stood out to us. It was a 3-bedroom, 2-bathroom brick townhouse with a basement just outside of metro Atlanta. Because Faith and I courted with the intent to marry, it was important to have her opinion on the purchase of a home she would be living in once we got married. And she loved it! I was ready to make an offer and live out the American dream. Unfortunately, things didn't go as planned. I received a phone call from the loan officer who informed me that upon further review of my finances, I would not be approved for a mortgage loan while my student loans were in forbearance. Confused by the information I just heard, I asked, "why?" The loan officer politely stated something to this effect: "forbearance indicates a hardship of some sort and if you cannot make payments on your student loans, the lender will not be confident you will be able to make mortgage payments either." I was devastated. The only way to finance a home was to take my student loans out of forbearance and to start making minimum payments. It was at this point that I began to realize firsthand the effects of being in debt.

Having debt can also affect your ability to buy a home if your debt-to-income (DTI) ratio is too high. Remember the debt-to-GDP ratio used by economists and investors to evaluate a country's ability to pay back its debt? Well, the debt-to-income ratio is used by mortgage lenders to determine a person's ability to repay his/her mortgage debt. To calculate your DTI ratio, simply add all your monthly debt payments and divide it by your gross monthly income. For example, let's say you have the following expenses:

$1,100/month as an estimated mortgage payment
$300/month for an auto loan
$450/month for your remaining debts

Your monthly debt payments would be $1,850 ($1100 + $300 + $450 = $1,850). If your gross monthly income is $5,000, then your DTI ratio would be 37% ($1,850 is 37% of $5,000). Generally, if your DTI ratio is above 36% it will be difficult to qualify for a mortgage.

The Government Can Garnish Your Wages

Many people are aware that the creditor of a financed or leased vehicle can repossess (repo) it if a person fails to make payments on the vehicle according to his/her financing agreement. The creditor has the right to do this without going to court or warning you in advance.

Similarly, a mortgage lender can foreclose (or take possession) on a home if a person fails to make payments per the mortgage agreement. But did you know the government can also garnish your wages for defaulting on your federal student loans? Wage garnishment occurs when a court issues an order for your employer to withhold or deduct a certain amount of money from your paycheck and send it directly to the lending institution until the debt is paid off. Pretty intrusive, I'd say. Below is an excerpt from FAFSA's website regarding defaulting on student loans.

> Default is a term used to classify your loans if you fail to repay your loan according to the terms agreed to when you signed your promissory note. For the FFEL and Direct Loan programs, default occurs if you fail to make a payment for 270 days if you repay monthly (or 330 days if your payments are due less frequently). It is important to make sure your loans do not become defaulted. If they do default, national credit bureaus may be notified, which may affect your credit rating for as long as seven years. This will make it difficult for you to borrow money from a bank to buy a car or a house. The Internal Revenue Service can withhold your U.S. individual income tax refund and apply it to the amount you owe, or the agency holding your loan might ask your employer to deduct payments from your paycheck. Also, you may be liable

for loan collection expenses. If you return to college, and you are in default, you're not entitled to receive additional federal student aid. Legal action also might be taken against you.[3]

Creditors Can Come After Your Assets When You Die

There are some people who believe it's okay to take their debt with them to the grave. These individuals throw in the towel and never truly put up a fight. Their decision is largely based on the assumption that their debt will not be passed on to their family members when they die. So, they go on to live their lives making minimum payments. Maybe their spouse never co-signed the loan, so they think they're in the clear. But if your spouse is a joint account holder on your debt or if you live in a community property state then he/she will be held liable. Whatever the case, because there are many, what they fail to realize is that creditors can come after your assets when you die.

Your assets classify anything you own (I will discuss assets in more detail later). If you planned to leave anything (property, cash, investments, etc.) behind for your heirs (relatives or anyone important to you), but you had outstanding debt at the time of your death, guess what could happen? Your assets could be eaten up by your debts! "How," you might ask? When a person dies, an estate is created. An estate is all the money and possessions owned by a person at death. While creditors may not be able to go after your spouse or children to collect debt payments in certain circumstances, they can go after the assets within your estate. The reason is that your estate becomes responsible for your debts upon death. It will be used to pay off all remaining bills and any debts you have outstanding, leaving your family less than what you had hoped to give them.

Now, if you don't have intentions to leave anything valuable for your heirs then disregard. However, I have a hunch you're wiser than that. We should all desire to build a legacy that our family can be proud of and one that will impact the generations after us. It is important to note that the concept of legacy goes beyond a plan to leave behind physical assets. Earlier in the chapter, I mentioned the integrity and honor behind paying off your debt. We should all desire to leave a legacy of character and of core values. Stand behind the promise you made when you signed the promissory note to pay off your debt. Leave a good name and a good reputation that will last long after you depart from this earth. You worked all your life for this. Do not allow debt to rob you of this opportunity.

Debt and Mental Health

While the effects of being in debt are most often seen with respects to the external consequences, there are also internal consequences worthy of being discussed. The reality is, debt is about much more than just money. There is a psychological, emotional, and mental aspect to debt and money that we have all experienced before in some way, shape, or form.

For a long time, conversations about money have been considered a taboo topic in the workplace and even amongst peers in social settings. Unfortunately, talking about debt has also fallen under that same stigma. Many individuals feel a sense of shame from being in debt and prefer not to think about it. This keeps them from having honest conversations about their debt and causes them to internalize their emotions. The result is often a perpetual cycle of poor financial behavior that leads to further debt. These behaviors can range from not opening bank statements, to deferring loans, to not sticking to a budget, and using credit cards on impulse.

Some common psychological and emotional issues associated with debt include depression, regret, anxiety, stress, resentment, anger, frustration, denial, fear, shame, embarrassment, and guilt. Can you relate to any of those? A study by Gathergood (2012) found that individuals who struggle to pay off their debt are more than two times as likely to experience worse psychological health, including depression and anxiety.[4] Similarly, a 2012 study in the *European Journal of Public Health* concluded that debt was one of the major risk factors for common mental disorders (CMD). The authors specifically stated the following in their research: "Adults in debt were three times as likely than those not in debt to have CMD. The increased likelihood of CMD among those in arrears (with outstanding payments) was found for all CMD and was irrespective of the source of debt - housing, utilities, and purchases on credit."[5]

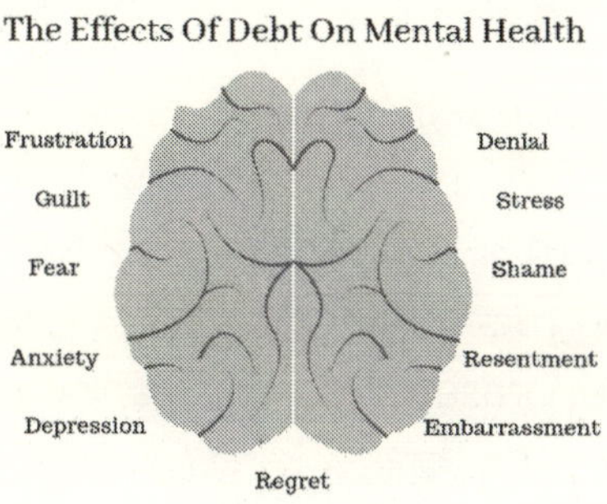

Figure 1.

Being in debt can be incredibly stressful. According to the 2017 "Stress in America" survey conducted by the American Psychological Association (APA), financial stress is one of the top causes of stress in Americans.[6] And usually, the first thing people neglect is their health when faced with financial burdens. The financial stress of being in debt can lead to a vast array of health issues as individuals become overwhelmed and lose a sense of control over their lives.

Because of the strong correlations between debt and mental health, it is not enough to simply learn how to cope positively with it. You must get out of debt and do everything in your power to stay out of it!

Now, let's debunk some of the common myths and misconceptions adapted by many regarding debt.

Myths About Debt

MYTH: DEBT IS NORMAL. THERE'S NO OTHER WAY BUT TO BORROW MONEY
TRUTH: YOU *CHOOSE* TO BORROW BUT *YOU DON'T HAVE TO*

Who told you borrowing money was the only way? Ever wonder why you receive so many credit card offers in the mail and see advertisements to finance the latest model vehicle during every television commercial break? The lending institution is a business. The industry spends billions of dollars researching the spending habits of individuals and billions of dollars in marketing strategies to entice you. Your loan is an asset in their account, and they are counting on you to make them rich. They are banking on the fact that you cannot delay gratification long enough to save for what you want. However, if you can spend years making minimum payments, you can also save money for a specific amount of time until you have the cash to pay for the items you want! It may take you longer to obtain it, but when you pay for it with your money, it's yours. You will no longer have to worry about anyone breathing down your neck to collect payments every month. You will no longer have to pay more than what your item, education, or car is worth. By doing this, you take back the control from the lending institutions who prey on your weakness of making impulsive purchases without first having the money to do so.

Secondly, many people believe that the only way to

fund college is by taking out a loan. Contrary to popular belief, that is not the only way! Before college begins, make applying for scholarships your full-time job in the summer. Earning three scholarships in the amount of $1,000/each is much more than you can earn working a regular minimum wage job. Here are two great resources where you can find tons of scholarship opportunities, grants, and prizes:

- The Ultimate Scholarship Book 2019 on Amazon
- Myscholly.com

An additional way to save on college tuition, along with room and board expenses, is to attend a community college while living at home. A community college will help to satisfy general education requirements before transitioning to a 4-year university, saving you tens of thousands of dollars. Lastly, working throughout college is another way to cover any added expenses. We must rid ourselves of the idea that debt is normal, and that borrowing is the only way. It's not! Choose to be free. It is within your power to do so.

> **MYTH**: I WILL NEVER BE DEBT FREE. IT WILL ALWAYS BE A PART OF MY LIFE
> **TRUTH**: YOU *CAN* MAKE THE DECISION **TODAY** TO GET OUT OF DEBT

Most people consider debt to be a normal part of life. Those people become overwhelmed with the amount of debt they have and think it's impossible to ever be debt free. Do not believe the lie that you must be in debt your entire life. Being and remaining in debt is a decision. So is the choice to be free. Sure, the road to debt freedom is no sprint; it's a marathon. It's a journey that will cause you to evaluate what's most important to you. A wise person once said, "when you know better, you can do better." The imperative word is *can*. You can be debt free. You can begin to remove these chains of bondage; one step at a time, one loan at a time.

Critical Thinking Questions

1. What are some ways companies and/or lending institutions set up *traps* to lure people into debt?

2. What are some ways to avoid the financial *traps* set before us?

Chapter 3

STEP 1: DREAM
I Declare War

Yesterday, December 7, 1941 – a date which will live in infamy – the United States of America was suddenly and deliberately attacked by naval and air forces of the Empire of Japan. - Franklin D. Roosevelt

So, on December 8, 1941, the day after the crushing attack on Pearl Harbor, Congress accepted the president's request to declare war on Japan.

Before you heal someone, ask him if he's willing to give up the things that made him sick. - Hippocrates

BEFORE I WALK YOU THROUGH THE 7 Bulletproof Steps to Debt Freedom, I must address the one factor that will determine how successful you will be on your journey – your choices. They can be springboards that propel you to heights you never thought you would reach. Or, they can be shackles that keep you enslaved to the endless, exhausting cycle of the Rat Race. I want you to become debt free. I really do. That's why I wrote this book. However, none of the steps discussed in these chapters will matter if you have not made the decision for yourself to get out of debt and stay out of it. I know there may be guilt and shame associated with your debt. You may have made some bad financial mistakes in the past. We all have. But do not allow them to define you. Today is a new day. It's a new beginning. You have been given another opportunity to make better choices and choose freedom. I developed a mantra, a war cry, if you will, for you to speak over yourself on your journey to debt freedom. It will help you combat negative thoughts that will try to take you off course and serve to encourage you to persevere until the end. I want you to repeat it any time you feel doubt, shame, guilt, worry, or fear rear their ugly heads. This is your Debt-Free Mantra (War Cry)!

DEBT-FREE MANTRA (WAR CRY)

My debt does not define who I am.
I forgive myself for all my past financial mistakes.
I own up to them and take full responsibility for
where I am now.
I make the vow to address them and move forward
with better money decisions.
My debt is costing me my freedom and today is the
day I say enough is enough.
I take control of my finances.

I have what it takes.
I am willing.
I will be debt free.

So, don't dwell on the past. You are not heading in that direction. I want you to be forward-focused. I dare you to dream.

STEP 1: DREAM

Your journey begins the moment you decide you no longer want to be where you currently are. - Anonymous

Dream? You're probably wondering why the first step toward debt freedom is to dream. It would seem that the most logical first step is to start crunching the numbers on the amount of debt you've amassed into some fancy calculator. "How can you start your journey without first knowing the numbers?" one may ask. You may not know the exact amount you owe. You may just have a rough idea. But do you think that would make a difference? I would contend that the reason most people have not started their journey to debt freedom or remained committed on their journey is not because they do not know how much they owe, but because they have failed to dream. Now what exactly do I mean by *dream*? I'm glad you asked!

To *dream* is to have a strongly desired goal or purpose. It is more than wishful thinking. It's more than an idea. It is your *WHY*. It is no coincidence that civil rights activist Martin Luther King Jr.'s "I Have A Dream" speech from 1963 continues to resonate in the hearts of people all over the world today. The power of his dream over 50 years ago transcended time and gave us all insight into why he found it worth it to go to jail 29 times for a cause that would ultimately cost him his life. Likewise, your *WHY* is a very important part of your debt free journey. It is the reason you start, the reason you sacrifice, the reason you endure when life gets hard, the reason your spouse gets on board, and so much more.

Before Faith and I tied the knot, it was important for us to attend premarital counseling with our pastors. This was a crucial part of our preparation before one of the biggest decisions of our lives. Our first counseling session was centered on the topic of the *purpose* of our marriage. What were we looking to accomplish by joining together as husband and wife? What did we want people to think of when they thought of the Jean-Louis family? We were given the assignment to discuss these questions and return with an answer at the following session. After much thought and prayer, we knew we wanted to have a large family and be a family that gives generously to others. Not only did we want to give monetarily, but we also wanted to give of our time. During our conversations, it became clear that the biggest barrier to us living out our God-given purpose was our debt. In regard to giving monetarily, our debt was a barrier for obvious reasons. How could we give generously with nearly $2,000 in monthly minimum debt payments? Regarding our time, we would be forced to spend the majority of it working to pay off this seemingly insurmountable amount of debt for the foreseeable future rather than on the people and the causes that were important to us.

Below is an activity Faith and I did chronicling how we spent our time. This would be a great activity for you to do as well!

List 3-5 things you enjoy doing. Create another line at the end of your list and include work. Next to each item on your list, indicate how many hours per week (or per month) you currently spend doing those activities.

This is what our list looked like during our peak months.

Leo

ACTIVITY	HOURS SPENT EACH WEEK/MONTH
1. Playing basketball	2 hours/month
2. Dining Out	3 hours/month
3. Watching movies /shows/sports	4 hours/week
4. Work (including commute time)	60 hours/week

Table 1.

Faith

ACTIVITY	HOURS SPENT EACH WEEK/MONTH
1. Traveling	0 hours/month
2. Spending time with friends	4 hours/month
3. Going to restaurants	3 hours/month
4. Work (including commute time)	88 hours/week

Table 2.

When we first completed this activity, we were shocked. We knew we were spending quite a bit of time working, but it was a reality check to see just how little time we spent doing the things we loved. That is precisely when we began to DREAM.

My wife and I dreamt of what life would be like not having debt payments every single month. We dreamt of not having to work 9-5 jobs for the next 30 years of our lives. Our dreams were big. We dreamt of becoming financially independent and retiring early (well before 50 years of age). We dreamt of giving generously to others. We dreamt of changing our family tree and leaving a legacy for the generations after us. We dreamt of traveling the world. We dreamt of not having to say no to our kids in the future due to financial reasons. We dreamt of being able to care for our parents as they aged. We dreamt of not trading our time for money and living life on our own terms. Dreaming opened up a world of opportunities for us – ones that did not exist had we continued to accept the status quo that "debt was normal."

How to Get Your Spouse on Board

Do two people walk hand in hand if they aren't going to the same place? - Amos 3:3

If you are married, engaged, or have hopes of being married one day, I want to take the time to stress the importance of being on the same page with your spouse.

This is especially important when it comes to finances. Did you know that money fights are the second leading cause of divorce, following infidelity? A popular question we receive from folks seeking to become debt free is "How do you get your spouse on board?" This is a great question because there is NO WAY you can succeed if the two of you are not in agreement on a plan. Sure, we all come from different backgrounds. The way we grew up thinking about money and the way we have learned to view money is probably different. But how can two walk TOGETHER unless they BOTH AGREE? You will be heading in one direction, while the other is heading in the opposite. And, your debt will be a looming cloud over your family for the rest of your life.

☑ PRO TIP

How to reach the SAME goal?
DO NOT MAKE THE ONE-DEGREE MISTAKE!

Did you know that EVEN IF you are heading in a similar direction, you will still ultimately end up at a completely different target if you are not on the same EXACT page with your spouse?

The one-degree mistake states if you are merely ONE degree off to start with, after only a mile you will be off by 92.2 feet! If you continue this way, you will be even further apart the longer you venture on your journey!

THE ONE-DEGREE DIFFERENCE

Figure 1.

Faith and I actually had conversations about finance EARLY on before we got married. We were both in a lot of debt and she had $8,000 from Sallie Mae sitting in her checking account to fund her spending – just living her best life! When I asked her to return the money to Sallie Mae, she was shocked! She had been living comfortably knowing she had a pile of money she could access whenever she pleased. What she did not realize at the time were the inevitable negative effects of that decision. That $8,000 was accruing interest at a high variable interest rate (9% at the time) and would have cost us thousands of dollars more by the time we got married if she held onto it. However, after several conversations and some reluctance, she sent the money back to Sallie Mae. We are much closer to debt freedom because we got on the same page from the very beginning.

INSIDE SCOOP 

While Faith and I were courting, one of our dates was spent working on an essay for her scholarship application for her Masters of Nursing program. Thankfully, she was awarded that scholarship, which covered her entire master's program at Emory University – a cost of ~$80,000! Had she not received it, our total combined debt would have been north of $300,000 when factoring in interest! Thank God that's not the case!

Whether you are newly married and learning how to combine finances or have been married for a while and can't seem to break out of destructive spending habits, having honest conversations with your spouse about finances is a must. Become naked and unashamed with your money. Absolutely nothing should be hidden from your spouse regarding finances. Combine your finances. There should no longer be that individualistic mindset that screams "mine" once you get married. What's his is hers and what's hers is his. Then, you can begin to dream. Be honest. Listen intently. Be patient. Your spouse will get on board when they know their voice is being heard and their desires genuinely considered. *Establish a dream that connects the both of you.* This should be something meaningful and something you can work toward together. Trust me, you will need each other during the many highs and lows of this journey. Above all, you'll be able to tackle your debt much more effectively because two is always better than one.

Seek Accountability

On your journey to debt freedom, you will definitely need some accountability. Most people will not understand why you're making such drastic sacrifices and changes to become debt free. And, if their faces don't give it away right when you tell them, they are definitely thinking it or will joke about it later. A relentless debt-free journey is not the norm so do not be surprised if your desire to be debt free is not embraced by those around you. You may face judgment, condemnation, and potentially humiliation. As you embark on your journey, you would not believe how much negative comments can affect you. Our co-workers have made jokes on occasion about my wife and I bringing our lunches to work. After we had some victory and shared the joy of paying off debt on social media, some people still did not fully support us. In response to our post that went viral on Instagram, one person said "I mean, you paid off all of that debt in one year, but what do you have to show for it? A piece of paper?" I even had someone ask me, "How would you feel if you paid off all of this debt and then you died?" I kid you not, these are real-life examples! You can combat these trains of thought with positive affirmations. When someone says you're crazy for embarking on this journey, tell them they're crazy for choosing not to. When someone scoffs at the sacrifices you're making, remember you will have the last laugh when you're out of debt and they're still living paycheck to paycheck. Remind yourself that this season of your life is temporary and always think back to the reasons you started! But don't be surprised if you are met with similar resistance. In your moments of weakness, such comments or peer pressure can become a major cause of financial relapse. Accountability helps you process and withstand those comments with victory. This is exactly why you need a good team around you.

Faith and I have each other as accountability; if you're married your spouse should be your first source. We also have specifically chosen friends as accountability. There will be many times when you want to break your budget, give up, and choose a less committed route. It is through these seasons your accountability partners should give you the exact amount of support, encouragement, and tough-love you need to stick to your plan. How do you find accountability partners? It takes having an honest conversation about your debt with someone that is able to be direct with you and fully support your financial goals. It may be a family member, a co-worker, or someone at your local church. If you and your accountability partners are all newbies to the debt-free journey, you may want to add someone to your group who is a bit more seasoned. This might be a parent or even a financial coach.

Some of our friends knew we were on the debt-free

journey but had no idea just how much we were sacrificing and working to pay off our debt. Over time, many of them have joined us on the journey and have become additional accountability partners. They know we may not see each other as often because we're picking up extra shifts and they don't pressure us to spend money because they're trying to save as well. Instead, we think of innovative ways to have just as much fun. For example, we have potlucks to keep the cost of entertainment down. We exchange money saving tips and help each other navigate personal finance challenges. I get inspired when I see them putting their hands to the plow for their families and vice versa. That's exactly what you need – a group of individuals you can create a community with to help motivate you on your journey to debt freedom!

> *The future belongs to those who believe in the beauty of their dreams. - Eleanor Roosevelt*

I want you to dream. I want you to take a moment to picture what life would be like if you no longer had debt. How would you spend your money if you did not have to use a good chunk of it to pay your dues? What would you do if there were fewer restrictions on the amount of time you could spend doing the things you loved? What if you were so financially secure you forgot it was payday? I want you to write 3-5 individual and/or family dreams of yours. It may require some time and deep reflection, but I want you to be honest with what you want for your life and for your family. Do not skip this activity. It is STEP 1 on your journey to debt freedom and is essential to your overall victory.

<u>ACTIVITY: DREAM BIG</u>
Below are examples of our Large-Scale Dreams

Large Scale Dream: I dream of becoming financially independent and retiring early.

Large Scale Dream: I dream of being able to travel the world.

Large Scale Dream: Our dream is to give generously to others, both monetarily and with our time/resources.

What is/are your Large-Scale Dream(s)?

I dream of

_______________________________________.

My/Our dream is to

_______________________________________.

Establishing the *why* behind the *what* should give you enough motivation to act regardless of where you are on the journey or what your current financial position is. So, DREAM... that's where goals begin!

☑ <u>PRO TIP</u>

Share your DREAM and your goals with a few people you trust. They will hold you accountable and you will be much more likely to accomplish them.

Critical Thinking Questions

1. Like President Roosevelt, what do you think it will actually *take* for *you* to declare war on your debt? What is *your* Pearl Harbor? Please see the reference to Pearl Harbor at the beginning of the chapter.

2. The Constitution of the United States states that only Congress has the power to declare war in the same way that only *you* have the power to DREAM. How does having a DREAM (establishing your WHY) help you combat the pressures/attacks from the lending institutions to get you into debt?

The BULLETPROOF Steps in Review

STEP 1: DREAM

Establish your reason(s) for wanting to be debt free. This is the *why* behind the *what*. Your DREAM is the reason you start your journey, the reason you do not quit, the reason your spouse gets on board, and so much more! This is the first step toward debt freedom.

CHAPTER 4

STEP 2: KNOW HOW MUCH YOU OWE

Don't Shoot Without a Target

When a sniper takes a shot, there are countless variables to consider before squeezing the trigger – wind speed, wind direction, range, target movement, mirage, light source, temperature, barometric pressure, and that's just the beginning. The work that goes into getting a good position to take a shot is immense. By tracking enemy movements, snipers wait patiently for the unsuspecting soldiers to present the opportunity for a perfect shot. An officer taking a break to smoke a cigarette, a pilot flight-checking his helicopter, an armed guard on patrol – these are all targets of opportunity.[1] - Robert Valdes

Let no debt remain outstanding, except the continuing debt to love one another, for whoever loves others has fulfilled the law.
- Romans 13:8 NIV

ONCE YOU'VE ESTABLISHED YOUR WHY by dreaming of what life could be without debt, the next step is to actually know how much you owe. Below are steps to guide you in establishing all the details and particulars of your debt:

A. Know how much you owe: part of knowing how much you owe is also knowing who you owe. The average person has debt from multiple lending institutions so it's important to know who services your loans and exactly how much you owe to each of them. Your debt-free goal amount, also known as your target amount, is the combined total you owe each institution. You cannot effectively strategize unless you know the exact amount you're up against.

B. Create an online account with each of the service providers for easy access to your accounts.

C. Bookmark each site or add them to your favorites as you will frequent these sites. This is where you will find all pertinent information regarding your loans, including loan amount, interest rates, loan terms, and repayment options.

D. List each lending institution with its corresponding debt and interest rate. In the case of student loans, it is not uncommon to have multiple loans with a specific lender. You can create an excel sheet with this information or simply insert a table (see the table below) on a Word document where you can visually see all of your information in one place.

E. Save the contact information of the lending institutions to your phone. I cannot tell you how many times we had to call and speak to a representative during our journey to ensure we had the most accurate information so we could plan our debt payments accordingly.

Below is a list of a few of our loans and their corresponding interest rates.

Table

Lending Institution	Amount of Debt	Interest Rate
Sallie Mae	1. $25,096.59 2. $22,934.54	9.5% 10%
Discover	3. $22,213.86	9.49%
Great Lakes	4. $4,952.79	6.84%
Fedloan Servicing	5. $20,858.31	6.55%

Table 1.

Some people have defaulted on their loans and their accounts may have been taken over by a collection agency. The specific details of these loans might be difficult to gather initially, especially if years have passed by. However, this is not an excuse to overlook those loans or to think they have magically disappeared. The government has developed a way for you to gather this information. As required by federal law, the three major credit bureaus – TransUnion, Equifax, and Experian – will provide you with a free annual credit report where you can verify your accounts for accuracy and view public records such as collection agency actions. You can access one free copy of your annual credit report from all three major credit bureaus at www.annualcreditreport.com.[2]

☑ **PRO TIP**

-Dioni Wise

You can obtain one free credit report from one of the three major credit bureaus every four months (January, May, September) or get all three at once during your free annual credit report.

Go to each of the sites below to get your one free copy during those specific months to access your reports throughout the year; it does not matter which order you choose to access them.

TransUnion: January **Equifax:** May **Experian:** September

A Tale of Two Stories

It is much easier to continue making minimum monthly payments and remain in your comfort zone than to make a radical change that will alter the lifestyle you've become accustomed to over the years. After all, your payments are "affordable," right? One question I like to ask those who are in debt is, "How much is your debt costing you?" Do you have any idea? This is where the category you listed in the table above titled *interest rates* factors in. Lending institutions would have no reason to let you borrow money if interest rates did not exist. In exchange for a loan, the lending institution receives a guaranteed return in the form of the interest they collect on your loan. As mentioned earlier in the "Myths About Debt" section in Chapter 2, these lending institutions study the spending habits of consumers and prey on individuals just like you and me. They know the average consumer cannot delay gratification long enough to save for what he/she wants. Furthermore, they know the chances of you paying off your balance in full at the end of the month is slim to none. The end result is thousands of dollars into their bank accounts, and never into yours.

In the book *Cashflow Quadrant* by Robert Kiyosaki, I learned one of the most valuable lessons about debt and wealth in two terms: assets and liabilities. In simple terms, an asset encourages cash flow which generates money *into* your pocket, while a liability hinders cash flow and demands money to come *out of* your pocket. An asset is an economic benefit to you. Examples of assets include, but are not limited to, cash, real estate, stocks, bonds, antiques, and mutual funds. A liability is an economic obligation you have to someone else. Examples of liabilities include, but are not limited to, credit card debts, student loans, personal loans, your financed cell phone, medical bills, and auto loans. If you take out a loan it becomes a liability as you would now be obligated to pay the financial institution the sum of money you borrowed, including any added interest. To better grasp this concept, you must have a good understanding of your personal financial statement. A financial statement is a formal record of the financial activities of a person, business or other entity; it includes at minimum an income statement (income and expenses) and a balance sheet (assets and liabilities). What's even more important to know is that there are always two sets of financial statements working simultaneously: yours and the banks (see the diagram below).

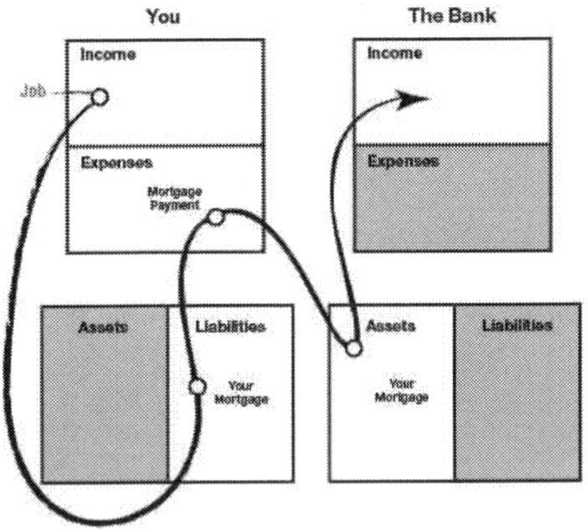

Figure 1. Retrieved from https://www.richdad.com/resources/rich-dad-financial-education-blog/november-2017/are-you-stuck-in-the-holiday-rat-race[3]

If you follow the arrow on the diagram above from the starting point of your income, your personal financial statement will tell a story. You produce the income through your job. In this example, you finance the purchase of a home and obtain a mortgage (liability). That mortgage is an expense to you in the form of monthly mortgage payments, resulting in cash flow **out of** your account. Are you still with me? If you continue to follow the arrow from the last reference point of the mortgage payment under the expense category, you will see the story your debt (in this case, your mortgage) tells regarding the lending institution's financial statement. Did you notice the difference? Your mortgage payment actually becomes an asset in the bank's financial statement! Why? Remember what the definition of an asset is? An asset cash flows money into your pocket. This is precisely what occurs if you continue to follow the arrow to the end. While your debt is taking money out of your pocket, it is adding money into the accounts of the banks. You are making them rich! This is the tale of two stories. Let us take a closer look at how interest rates work. Remember, there would be no incentive for the bank to let you borrow money if they did not charge you interest.

The Numbers Don't Lie

I've heard many people say they will let the government pay off their student loans by applying for the Public Service Loan Forgiveness (PSLF) program. This program allows for certain not-for-profit and government employees to apply to have their federal student loans eradicated (forgiven) after 10 years (120 months) of *qualifying payments* (payments made on a Direct federal loan under an income-driven repayment plan while working full-time for a public service employer). However, before rushing to apply for such programs, let us first discuss the effects of interest on your loans. Interest on your loans can either be simple interest or compound interest.

Simple Interest

The formula for simple interest is: **A = P(1+rt)**

>   **Where:**

> **A** = the future amount of the loan, *including interest*

> **P** = the principal loan amount

> **r** = the annual interest rate (decimal form)

> **t** = the number of years the money is borrowed for

To help you understand how interest rates work, I will walk you through a quick example. This example should challenge those who think being in debt for 10 years and waiting for the government to forgive their loans is a good idea. Using the simple interest rate formula, let's calculate the amount of money you would pay over this 10-year time-frame of 120 payments as is the requirement for this program. In this example, let's say your outstanding student loan balance is $30,000 and your interest rate is

6.5%. The purpose of this example is to calculate the amount of interest you would accrue on your loan over a 10-year time-frame and will not factor in any monthly payments for simplicity purposes. With simple interest, interest builds on the principal. See the illustration below.

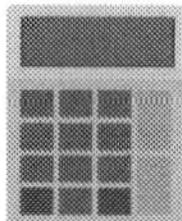

www.freedomisachoicemvt.com

Figure 2.

By the end of the 10 years, you would have paid $19,500 in interest alone! Your total payment by the end of year 10, would be a whopping $49,500 for a loan you took out with an original balance of $30,000, assuming no minimum payments are made. Now, if you took that same loan and paid it off in five years, rather than 10, the total interest paid would be $9,750 (half). Paying it off in three years would result in a total interest of $5,850. I strongly believe the lending institutions want you to take as long as possible to pay them back. The longer you take, the more money in their pocket!

Compound Interest

Unfortunately, the interest rate on most loans is not calculated as simple interest. Most loans are calculated as compound interest. With compound interest, interest builds on both the principal amount and the previously earned interest. The interest gets calculated on the new principal amount/outstanding balance until the loan is repaid. Here is an illustration on how compound interest would be calculated over the initial 10-year period using the same principal amount and interest rate that were used under the simple interest example. Likewise, this illustration assumes you are not making regular monthly payments for simplicity purposes.

Year 1: $30,000 x 6.5% = $1,950
Year 2: $31,950 x 6.5% = $2,076.75
Year 3: $34,026.75 x 6.5% = $2,211.73

Year 4: $36,238.48 x 6.5% = $2,355.50
Year 5: $38,593.98 x 6.5% = $2,508.60
Year 6: $41,102.58 x 6.5% = $2,671.66
Year 7: $43,774.24 x 6.5% = $2,845.32
Year 8: $46,619.56 x 6.5% = $3,030.27
Year 9: $49,649.83 x 6.5% = $3,227.23
Year 10: $52,877.06 x 6.5% = $3,437.00
Total = $56,314.06 (principal $30,000 + interest $26,314.06)

The total interest accrued on this loan after 10 years would be $26,314.06 compared to the total interest accrued after 10 years using the simple interest formula ($19,500). Of course, if you are making regular monthly payments on your loans, the total amount of interest will be lower because the remaining principal will be decreasing at each level. The effects of the interest, however, still stand true.

It is important to ask your lender if interest on your loans accrue yearly, monthly, or daily. In the example above, we calculated compound interest based on a yearly accrual. However, in the case of most student loans, you will find that interest is accrued daily. To obtain more accurate numbers based on the daily accrual of interest on your loans using compound interest, use the formula below.

The formula for compound interest is $A = P(1+r/n)^{(nt)}$.

Where:

A = the future amount of the loan, *including interest*

P = the principal loan amount

r = the annual interest rate (decimal form)

n = the number of times that interest is compounded per year

t = the number of years the money is borrowed for

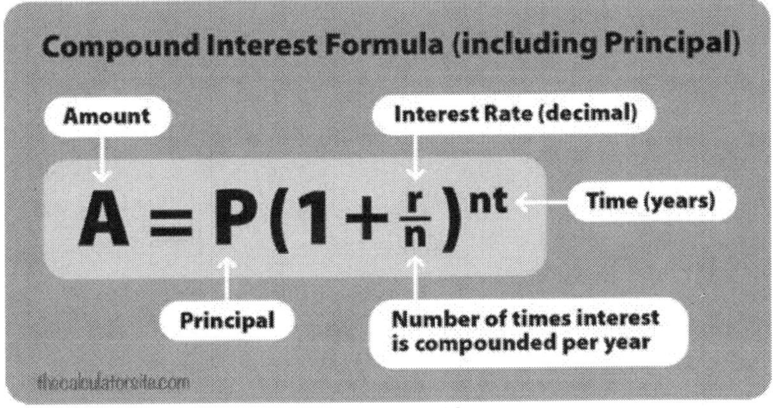

Figure 3. Retrieved from https://www.thecalculatorsite.com/articles/finance/compound-interest-formula.php[4]

If interest compounds daily, the formula would be A= p(1+r/365) $^{(10*365)}$. Now, let's see the effect of compounding interest on your loans based on a daily accrual. Don't get overwhelmed at the equation. I will walk you through it so that you understand it and can easily input your own numbers! Let's plug in the numbers using the same principal balance, interest rate, and a 10-year time frame. You will need a calculator.

See the illustration below.

www.freedomisachoicemvt.com

Figure 4.

If you do not have a scientific calculator, you can do a simple google search by typing "exponent calculator from calculator.net" to obtain the value of the exponent (^) in the equation above.[5]

How much is your loan costing you? Insert your numbers into the equation A= p(1+r/365) $^{(10*365)}$. Follow the steps line by line. Compare different time frames such as 10 years vs. 5 years vs. 3 years. Are you okay with paying all of that extra money to the lending institution? Could that money not serve you and your family better if you no longer had debt payments?

For an estimated idea of how long it will take you to pay off your loans while making your current minimum payments, you can do a simple Google search by typing "money under 30 loan payoff calculators." This loan payoff calculator will also allow you to see how much interest you will pay over that time frame.[6]

If looking at the amount of interest you would owe over the life of your loan does not stir you to get angry at your debt and make you want to start selling everything you own to pay it off, let's consider this. An article published by Annie Nova of CNBC titled "Just 96 of 30,000 People Who Applied for Public Service Loan Forgiveness Actually Got It" reported this alarming finding – the Education Department reported it has forgiven fewer than 100 people's loans under the Public Service Loan Forgiveness program in 2017. Did you read how many people applied? Nearly 30,000 borrowers have applied for this program and only 96 people have been released from their debt. ONLY NINETY-SIX! "That means less than 1% of the people who applied actually got it," Annie Nova writes. Another way of phrasing this is to say 99% of the applicants who applied were rejected! The article gives an example of a music teacher in Oklahoma, who after paying on her student loans for

10 years while believing she was on her way to debt forgiveness, was told she did not qualify because she had the wrong type of federal student loans. Can you believe that? In fact, many people who believe they are in the program are finding out the hard way that they do not qualify for what seems to be various technical reasons. The article goes on to say that the Consumer Financial Protection Bureau reported that student loan servicers are starting to delay and/or deny access to the program as well. Reports also show the White House submitted a budget proposal to de-fund the Public Service Loan Forgiveness program in the recent past that did not make it into law.[7] How much confidence do you have in the government that this program will even be around 10 years from now? Just ask the baby boomers their thoughts on the looming uncertainty of social security benefits.

Now, let's tie this all together and give you even more reasons why you need to get rid of your debt and do so immediately!

The Rule of 72

The rule of 72 is a quick and well-known mathematical formula used in finance to estimate the number of years it would take your invested money to double at a given fixed annual rate of return. This rule helps to further demonstrate the power of compounding interest. Not only can you use this formula for investments, but you can also use it to calculate how long it would take your debt to double if you failed to address it aggressively. Here's the formula.

Y = 72/r

where **Y** is the number of years it would take, and **r** is the fixed interest rate.

Let's say you have $50,000 of debt with an average interest rate of 8%. Your calculation would be as follows:

Y = 72/8

It would take your debt approximately nine years to double (72/8 = 9).

In other words, your $50,000 debt would double to $100,000 in nine years (assuming you are not aggressively paying it off).

Now input your specific numbers into the equation:

Y = 72/___.

If you have multiple loans with different interest rates, simply take the average of those interest rates and insert it into the equation.

How many years would it take for your total amount of debt to double?

Let us now take it a step further. Remember what was discussed in the section on assets and liabilities earlier in this chapter? Assets cash flow money into your pocket while liabilities take money out of your pocket. I also explained that there are two financial statements in play at the same time when it comes to your debt: yours and the banks.

Your loans are liabilities for you, but they are assets to the lending institutions. So, can you guess how they're applying this rule to your loans? They are using it to estimate how long it will take for their assets (your loans) to double! By not aggressively paying off your debt you are helping the banks double the amounts on their financial statements and not yours! So, how long do you plan to take to pay off your loans now that you are aware of these concepts? Not too long, I hope!

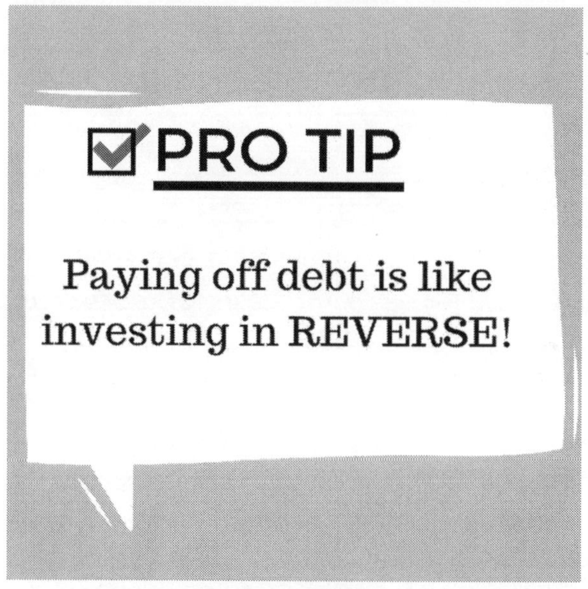

Pay Off Debt FIRST or Invest

Should you aggressively pay off your debt first or should you start investing? This is the million-dollar question. The crux of this common dilemma is what you should do with any extra money you have (you should always make the minimum payments on your debts in either case). You may have heard convincing arguments for both sides and are still unsure what to do. On one hand, those who advocate for investing in the stock market say it's the better option due to the power of compounding interest. They argue you could earn a higher return on investments than the interest you would save by paying off your debt first. On the other hand, those who advocate for paying off debt aggressively first say it's the better option because the return on paying down your debt is a guaranteed one.

Generally speaking, if the return on investments is higher than the interest you would save on paying off your debt, then you should invest. However, if you're paying more in interest than what you could earn in the stock market, then you should get rid of your debt first. For example, if you have a credit card with an interest rate above 15% (which is the case for most credit cards), then you should pay it off because the money you would save on interest is likely higher than what you would earn in the stock market. Sounds like a simple decision, right? Not quite. There are a few factors I would like you to consider that make the case for aggressively paying down debt first the better option. Here they are.

Risk: While those who advocate for investing focus on the return you could gain on your investments, they often leave out the potential risks involved when making such decisions. The truth is, all investments have some degree of risk. There is a level of uncertainty and potential for financial loss that needs to be accounted for. This is not the case for paying down debt.

Guaranteed return: Unlike other investments, the return on paying down your debts is a guaranteed one. Let's say you have a $25,000 loan with an interest rate of 8%. Once you pay off that debt, you have an immediate and guaranteed 8% return on your money. This is much safer than trying to pick out investments in the stock market. Don't believe me? See what billionaire owner and Shark Tank investor Mark Cuban had to say on the topic: "If you've got $25,000, $50,000, $100,000, you're better off paying off any debt you have because it's a guaranteed return."

Time: Time is the biggest variable when discussing the power of compounding interest so it makes sense that starting to invest early would give your money more time to grow. Proponents of investing say aggressively paying off debt first will cause you to miss out on valuable years when your money could be growing exponentially. However, they leave out one very important detail. Those who follow a plan to aggressively pay off their debt (such as the one described in this book) should not be in debt for as long as they make it seem. When you no longer have any debt payments, you should be able to double or even triple the amount you put toward investing. By doing this, you would make up for that lost time in the long run.

Figure 5.

*Pay off your debt first. Freedom from debt is
worth more than any amount you can earn.*
– Mark Cuban

When you make the decision not to pay off your debts aggressively first, you are essentially borrowing money to invest. Don't get me wrong, investing is an admirable aspiration and a key component to wealth building. However, this question is not about whether or not you should invest but rather *when* to invest. I believe investing should come after you have finished paying off all consumer debt with the exception of your mortgage. Once you are debt free, you will be unrestrained in the amount of money you can allocate toward investing. Not only will you recoup any time lost from not investing initially, but you will also eventually surpass the individual who decided to hold on to their debt and invest simultaneously.

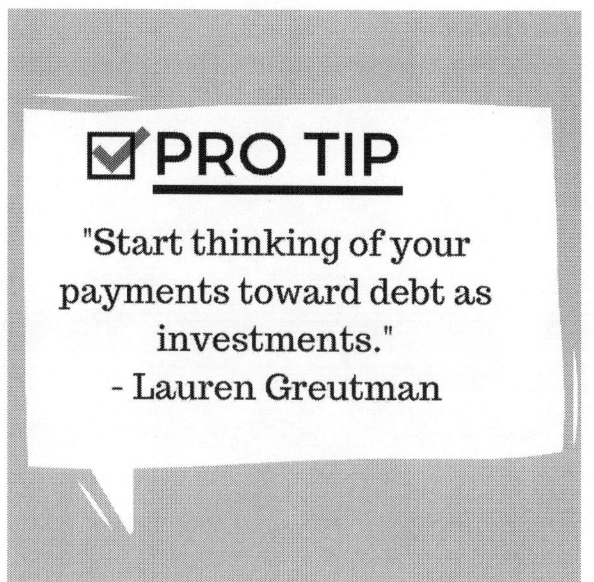

Conclusion

You have already established your *why* by dreaming and you now know how much you owe. It's time to combine BULLETPROOF STEP 1 and BULLETPROOF STEP 2. Now, I want you to create a goal for your DREAM component from STEP 1. Make sure that at least one of your goals includes your *debt-free goal amount* from BULLETPROOF STEP 2. Please see the SMART Goal activity below.

ACTIVITY: CREATE SMART GOALS

SMART is an acronym used to help guide your goal setting. They ensure your goals are clear and unambiguous so you can improve your chances of actually accomplishing them. I will explain what each letter of the acronym stands for below.

- **S**pecific – What do you want to do? Your goal should be as specific as possible.

- **M**easurable – How will you know when you've achieved it? Measurement will give you specific feedback and hold you accountable.

- **A**chievable – Is it in your power to accomplish it?

- **R**ealistic – Can you realistically achieve it?

- **T**ime – When exactly do you want to accomplish it? Do you have a time frame listed in your SMART Goal?

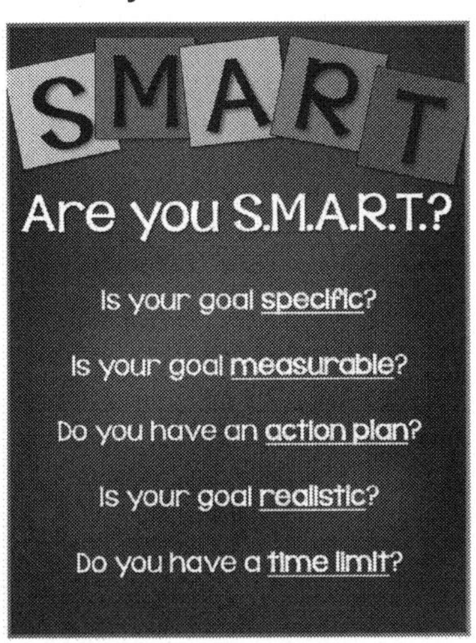

Figure 6. Retrieved from https://www.whatihavelearnedteaching.com/product/are-you-smart-goal-setting-lessons/ [8]

Part 1: List your large-scale dreams from Chapter 3.

____.

Part 2: Create a SMART Goal from your large-scale dream (make sure your goal is specific, measurable, achievable, realistic, and has a time frame).

____ .

Part 3: How will you accomplish your SMART Goal so your large-scale dream can become a reality?

____.

Please see the examples below:

List your large-scale dreams from Chapter 3	Create a SMART Goal from your large-scale dream (make sure your goal is specific, measurable, achievable, realistic, and has a time frame).	How will you accomplish your SMART Goal so your large-scale dream can become a reality?
I dream of becoming financially independent and retiring early.	In two years, I will pay off my credit cards and student loans totaling $211,089 to become debt free.	I will live below my means by following a strict budget and allocate extra money toward my debt.
I dream of being able to travel the world.	Within the next three years, I will travel to another continent at least once.	I will save $100 every month into a travel fund.
Our dream is to give generously to others, both monetarily and with our time.	We will give generously to others by sponsoring one family every Christmas.	Every month, we will save $25 into a giving fund.

Table 2.

☑ **PRO TIP**

Break your goals down into daily, weekly, or monthly attainable goals.

Set a date on your calendar to do a quarterly or mid-year review on your goals.

Critical Thinking Questions

1. Why is it important to know who you owe, your target amount, and the interest rates on your loans?

2. How do you find out the terms and repayment options for your loans?

The BULLETPROOF Steps in Review

STEP 1: DREAM

Establish your reason(s) for wanting to be debt free. This is the *why* behind the *what*. Your DREAM is the reason you start your journey, the reason you do not quit, the reason your spouse gets on board, and so much more! This is the first step toward debt freedom.

STEP 2: KNOW HOW MUCH YOU OWE

Identify your target number. This is your debt-free goal amount. List all of the lending institutions you owe, along with the current balance and interest rates for each loan. You cannot effectively strategize unless you know the exact amount you're up against.

Chapter 5
STEP 3: BUDGET
Strategy and Tactics

Military strategy and tactics are essential to the conduct of warfare. Broadly stated, strategy is the planning, coordination, and general direction of military operations to meet overall political and military objectives. Tactics implement strategy by short-term decisions on the movement of troops and employment of weapons on the field of battle. - Ronald E. Goodman

Perhaps the most legendary military commander in history was Alexander the Great, whose military strategies and tactics led him to never lose a battle in 15 years! Alexander the Great conquered most of the ancient world by outwitting the other nations with a few of the following strategies and tactics: the mobility of his army (to attack from the sides when least expected), having his soldiers strap their shields in a way that would take the weight around the shoulders so both hands could be free, and using 21-foot-long spears (known as a sarissa) that were far longer than the enemy's. His military genius was exemplary, so much so that his strategies and tactics are still studied in military academies to this day.

If you fail to plan, then you plan to fail.
-Benjamin Franklin

BY NOW YOU HAVE ESTABLISHED YOUR *WHY* FOR getting out of debt by dreaming (BULLETPROOF STEP 1) and you now know exactly how much you owe (BULLETPROOF STEP 2). It's time to start paying off your debt! Not so fast. In order to implement a successful plan to pay off your debt, you must first learn the crucial art of budgeting and master it. Failing to do so will cost you both time and money – two things that are vital on your journey to debt freedom. Benjamin Franklin said it best when he eloquently coined the phrase "If you fail to plan then you plan to fail." This is precisely what happens when you fail to establish a budget.

The word *budget* is often met with resistance and can leave a distasteful impression, particularly on those who are less familiar with the process and the benefit it offers. This word can seem scary, daunting, and restrictive, but it doesn't have to be this way! It should actually be far from it! A budget is an estimate of income and expenses over a set period of time; while a budget can serve many purposes, its ultimate goal is for you to make a plan for your money. Businesses use budgets to create goals and to assess the performance of the company financially (what is going out vs. what is coming in), thereby forecasting profitability. A personal or household budget is needed to give you financial direction and help you stay on track with your financial goals. Hence, a budget should work for you and not against you. Ever wonder what happened to all of your hard-earned money over the course of the month? Have you ever sat down to reflect and consider what you have to show for all of the hours you've worked and all of the money you've earned over this past year? Seriously, think about it! Does holding onto money feel more like a fruitless attempt to grasp oil with your hands? The primary goal of a budget is for you to plan where your money will go before you even receive your paycheck or direct deposit, instead of wondering where it all went by month's end. Without tracking what is coming in and going out you are unable to realistically and effectively manage your money.

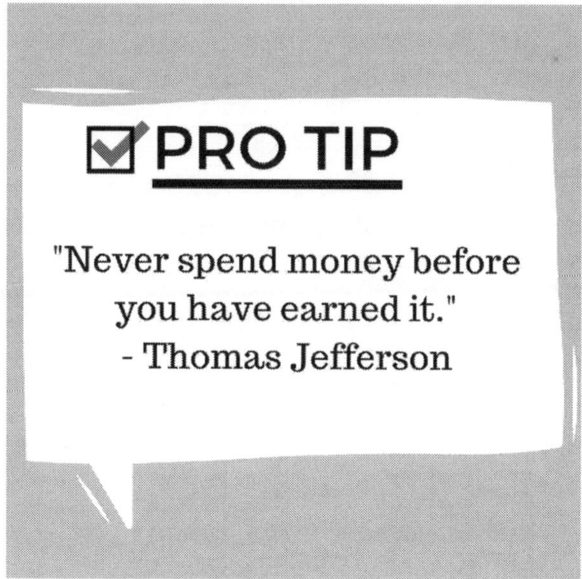

We are all creatures of habit. Relatively speaking, we tend to do the same things each day, week by week, month by month, etc. For example, we usually wake up around the same time each day, leave the house for our 9-5 jobs around the same time, make a quick stop for our usual morning coffee, and listen to the same genre of music. We then leave work, stop at the gym, return home for dinner, and maybe catch a few hours of our favorite TV shows or sports games before going to bed around the same time. We wake up just to follow the same pattern all over again. No, I do not know you personally, but how close was I to describing your routine? Of course, habits and routines are not inherently a bad practice. In fact, habits and routines are excellent practices when the focus is something positive, such as taking the time to read to your toddlers at night, exercising at least 3 days per week, drinking lots of water, or spending time in prayer. The issue arises when the habit or routine is one that is unhealthy and brings about a negative result, such as what is likely to happen when you don't budget – frivolous spending. If you don't budget, then you are most likely not tracking your spending. You may think you have a good grasp of your finances because you're still somehow remaining afloat and are able to "afford" your way of living, but what do you have to show for it? How much money do you have in your savings account? How much do you have in your investment accounts? For those of you reading with a decent amount in your savings or retirement accounts, you are probably pumping your chest and holding your head high at your perceived achievement. To you, I ask the question from Chapter 4: How much debt do you have, again? If you were to stop working today, how long could you survive without needing to receive a paycheck? What's your net worth? Your net worth is the best indicator of how well off you are financially. So, let's do a quick activity to calculate it.

ACTIVITY: CALCULATE YOUR NET WORTH

Your personal net worth is the value of all of the assets you own minus all of your outstanding liabilities (debts).

To calculate your net worth, do the following:

1. Make a list of all of your assets with their respective monetary value.

2. List all of your liabilities with their respective monetary value.

3. Next, plug your numbers into the following formula:

- **Assets – Liabilities** (debts) = **Net Worth**

For example, let's say your assets total $20,000 (savings, retirement account(s), antiques, etc.), but you have $37,000 of debt (the average student loan debt in 2018). Your net worth would be negative $17,000.

- $20,000 – $37,000 = -$17,000.

The average citizen does not think of their financial portfolio in terms of net worth. However, knowing your net worth is vital because it might be the single most important measure of your personal wealth. In other words, it is a snapshot of your current financial situation. You can track your net worth on a platform called Personal Capital (www.personalcapital.com) for free.

So, what's your net worth?

When Faith and I calculated our net worth at the beginning of our debt-free journey, we had a negative net worth of ~$342,000!

So, pump the brakes before you dismiss the recommendation of starting a budget. I can guarantee that you have money slipping through your hands as we speak because of your spending habits and you don't even know it! By tracking your spending, you will see the patterns and routines you have established in regard to your finances. Tracking your spending will also allow you to see if your spending habits line up with the goals you have for yourself and for your family. For example, is your goal to be debt free, but your spending habits reveal you're addicted to online shopping? Some of the most important areas I would suggest you start tracking are food, clothing, and entertainment. Do you know how much you spend each month in these categories?

Your Outcome With Money Won't Change Unless Your Mindset Does

One of my favorite books on finance is *The Millionaire Next Door* by Thomas J. Stanley and William D. Danko. The authors conducted years of research on the secrets of America's wealthy. Their results would surprise you! The spending habits of millionaires reveal a story that is far different from what is often portrayed on media platforms. Millionaires budget and control their expenses. They know this is imperative to their wealth building and this is an area they do not compromise on. They do not buy the highest priced items. They are not caught in the trap of consuming just to impress people. Rich people become rich and remain rich by living like they're broke. Broke people become broke and remain broke by living like they're rich. Their money habits and mindset around spending are just different. After all, they didn't become wealthy by doing what the average person does. The authors go on to say that many people could be wealthy but are not because of their mindset around spending. One thing I found particularly interesting is that millionaires know exactly how much they spend on each category of spending. According to the book, they know how much they spend on clothing, groceries, transportation, housing, utilities, entertainment, etc.[1] If you don't know how much money you're spending on each category, you're definitely not budgeting. And if you're not budgeting, your chances of being successful with money are significantly reduced. Let's change that!

Spending Triggers

It's very tempting to spend more than you earn, it's very understandable. But it's not a good idea. – Warren Buffett

While tracking your spending reveals what your spending patterns are and what you value most, it is equally important for you to know what your *spending triggers* are. Have you ever paused to think about what drives you to spend the way you do? Do you get a shopper's high? This is definitely a thing. Some people actually experience a high during the physical act of buying! For these individuals, shopping releases endorphins, a chemical in your brain that leads to feelings of happiness, even euphoria. Are you a sucker for sales and discounts? Some people feel good about being savvy shoppers. While this is definitely a good practice when you *need* something, buying a product or a service just because it's on sale is not. There's a reason Black Friday and its sister Cyber Monday are some of the biggest shopping days in America. Stores make it a point to direct your focus toward what you're saving rather than on what you're spending. And, we as the consumers have been tricked into doing the same. Think about this for a second. Haven't you noticed more store cashiers telling you how much you saved on your purchase? We completely disregard how much we're spending and focus solely on what we're saving! Is one of your triggers to spend out of envy? Do you get the urge to spend as soon as you see someone else with something desirable? This is a classic symptom of "Keeping up with the Joneses." Or, maybe you spend when you're stressed, bored, hungry, or depressed. Whatever your spending triggers are, identifying them and fighting against them is necessary if you want to win with your finances.

There are several habits you can develop to fight against those triggers once you identify them. If you have the urge to shop because of the shopper's high, engage in another activity that releases those same happy endorphins, like exercising. If you find yourself struggling to walk away from that 30% sale, remember this very important fact – you never save by spending. Another great tip to fight many common spending triggers is to challenge yourself to a *spending freeze*. Try a *no-spend* month except for your necessities. During that time period, record your feelings and experiences in a journal and you'll be amazed at what you learn about yourself. Identifying your spending triggers and learning how to deal with them will not only help you change your financial behavior, but it will also give you the discipline you need to remain steadfast on your journey to debt freedom.

How To Start A Budget

In the previous chapter, I introduced the term *income statement*, which is part of your financial statement – a formal record of the financial activities of a person, business or other entity. The income statement keeps a record of two categories – your income and your expenses. Before Faith and I got married, we decided to invest in our financial future by hiring a certified financial planner (CFP). A certified financial planner is an individual trained extensively in the areas of financial planning, taxes, estate planning and retirement, and insurance. We made sure to hire a fee-only fiduciary CFP, which simply means one who is obligated to operate solely in our interest without the added pressure of selling products. With the amount of debt we had, we knew it was extremely important for us to start making better financial decisions from the start of our marriage. Now, hiring a financial planner is not necessary to start a budget. I mention our CFP here to stress the importance of having a budget. It was one of the first things we were required to do when we established our business relationship. It provided both parties with a clear picture of our finances and our spending. Our CFP wanted to see where our money was going so she could better assist us. If someone trained this extensively in the areas of finance finds it important to budget, then it might be a great idea for you to adopt this practice as well.

To determine the income (Money IN) portion of your income statement, simply record your net pay for the month. Your net pay is the amount of money you take home each month from your paycheck, after taxes. Simply, look at your pay stubs or direct deposits from the last two pay periods and add it together to get your total income for the month if you get paid bi-weekly (if you get paid weekly, total the amount from each paycheck you receive in a month). If you work in sales with a commission-based service or are paid on an irregular income, then your net pay should come from your base salary. I would recommend starting by jotting this down on a single sheet of paper. That's how I began. The income portion of your income statement is now completed. Next, label a category titled expenses (Money OUT). Under this category, you will list out all of your monthly expenses. Some items on your list may be fixed and some may be variable, but I want you to list them all out – every single item! Once you list your income followed by your expenses, you will subtract your expenses from your income to determine how much money, if any, you have left over.

The equation is:

$$\text{Income} - \text{Expenses} = \text{Cash Flow}$$

Your cash flow can either be positive or negative. Here is a simple diagram explaining how to start a budget.

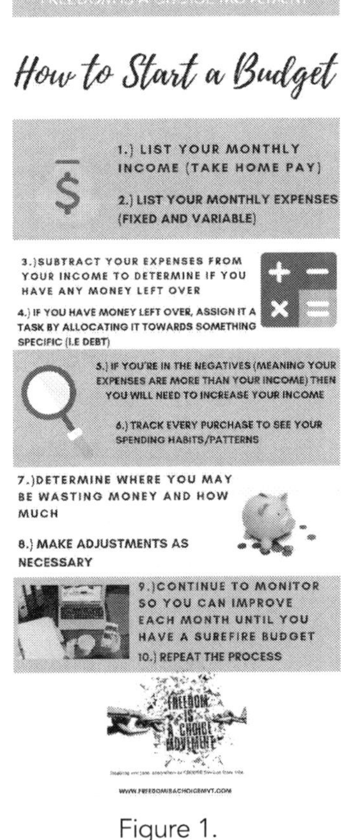

Figure 1.

Ideally, you want to be cash flow positive, meaning that after you have accounted for all of your expenses (i.e. all of your bills are paid and you factored in all of the money you spend during the month) there is money left over. This is the money you would use as an extra payment toward your debt. So, how does your income statement look? Are you cash flow positive or cash flow negative? I hope you are the former, however, it is very common not to be. If not, there's still hope for you. We will dive deeper into the adjustments you will need to make to increase your cash flow in Chapter 7. Now, let me show you the type of budget you will need on your journey to debt freedom – a *zero-based budget*.

In the previous section, I walked you through how to start your budget by listing your income and your current monthly expenses then subtracting your expenses from your income to determine your cash flow for the month. I recommend taking it a step further. You should assign every dollar you earn a *task* so that by the end of the month you have zero dollars left over. This is called a *zero-based budget* and it comes highly recommended by chief financial guru, Dave Ramsey. It simply means that you have to find a use for every dollar you receive in income. Generally speaking, this would include all monthly expenses and also any savings or debt payments. For example, if your monthly income is $3,000, then you want all of the line items in your budget to total $3,000, leaving you with zero at the end of the month. If you happen to receive $50 for your birthday or were awarded a bonus for meeting your company's goals this month, then you would need to assign that amount a *task* as well so that all money received in income is accounted for.

The equation for the zero-based budget is:

Income – Expenses = Zero

Of course, this does not mean you should keep a zero balance in your checking account every month (you should keep the minimum required balance in your checking account at all times so you are not assessed any fees). With this kind of budget, you do not carry over last month's budget automatically into the next month. Additionally, the line items in your budget can change on a month-to-month basis, as needed, as long as you establish it beforehand. For example, if you pay your auto insurance once a year or once every six months then you would adjust your budget for the particular month your bill is due. Once that month is over, you can remove that category. You would do the same for the month following the $50 you received for your birthday and the bonus check you received. Having a *zero-based budget* ensures that every dollar is accounted for, thereby eliminating the stress and worry about where your money is going and truly giving you control over your finances.

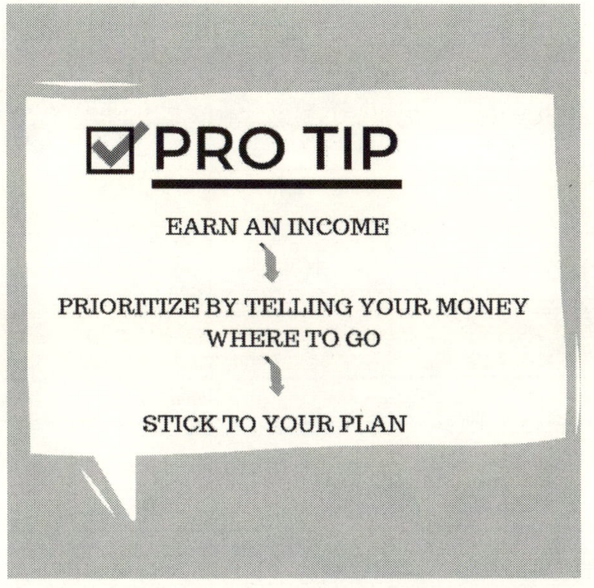

Just how conservative should your spending be per category if you're on the journey to debt freedom? Let's use the example of a single person who earns a salary of $50,000/year. After taxes and health insurance premiums, your estimated income should be ~$3,000/month or $1,500 bi-weekly. The chart below details the recommended percentages to allocate toward each category of spending while on your debt-free journey. Please be advised that this is a general guideline and it is very conservative in nature in order to maximize the amount of money you could put toward your debt.

Survival Budget for Your Debt-Free Journey

Category	Percentage of Overall Spending	The Dollar Amount Allocated
Giving: Tithes, offering, giving to charity, random acts of kindness	10%	$300/month
Food: Groceries	8-10%	$300/month based on 10%
Housing: Rent or mortgage payments (15-year loan)	25-28%	$750/month based on 25%
Clothing/Personal Care: Hair, nails, etc. *It is not necessary to use this category every month while working to pay off your debt.*	3%	$90/month
Transportation: Gas, auto insurance, routine maintenance, etc.	10%	$300/month
Utilities: Gas, electric, water, garbage/sewer, etc.	8-10%	$240/month

Miscellaneous: Wedding gifts, baby showers	2%	$60/month
Debt: Auto loans, student loans, personal loans, mortgage, etc.	30-32%	$960/month based on 32%

Table 1.

Your debt-free budget should include the basic necessities of food, shelter, clothes, transportation, and utilities. These are your needs versus your wants. Your food category is for groceries and should not include restaurants; I recommend cooking at home while on your debt-free journey (I elaborate more on this in Chapter 7). The *shelter* category is the amount you pay for the cost of housing and that should be no more than *25-28% of your monthly take-home pay*; if you have a mortgage, it should be no more than *25-28% of your monthly take-home pay on a 15-year mortgage.* The reason for choosing a 15-year mortgage over a 30-year mortgage is simple. Why would you want to be in debt for 30 years? If you currently have a 30-year mortgage, you can either choose to refinance it into a 15-year loan or pay it off as if it were a 15-year loan. Be aware that this will increase your monthly mortgage payments. If your newly calculated monthly mortgage payment is estimated to be more than 25-28% of your monthly take-home pay, then you have too much *house* and should strongly consider making some changes. I will discuss this in more detail in Chapter 7. For the clothing category, you probably have more than enough already to keep this category at the bare minimum until you are debt free. Your transportation category includes any form of transportation (bus passes, subway passes, etc.) you use for your basic daily travel needs. If you have a vehicle, this includes car insurance and gas for your car. Utilities would include your water, electricity, and gas bills.

The Survival Budget is a recommended list of percentages for you to start your budget. You can adjust the percentages according to your personal needs as necessary. For example, if you find that 10% is too much for food then you can lower the percentage and increase the percentage in another category where you don't quite have enough. Ideally, you would increase the percentage going toward your debt!

One important category not listed here is your emergency fund. Before aggressively attacking your debt, I strongly recommend you have a starter emergency fund in place. The sample survival budget listed above assumes your starter emergency fund is already completed, although I know this may not be the case for everyone at this point in the journey. If you do not yet have one, that's okay. To start your budget, add a starter emergency fund category to your list. Stop all *extra* payments toward debt and put it toward your starter emergency fund instead until you reach $1,000 (I recommend a different amount for special circumstances in the next chapter). You should continue making minimum payments on your debt, but any extra money should be put toward your starter emergency fund until you have it fully funded. Once you have a starter emergency fund of $1,000, any extra cash you have would then go toward your debt. In Chapter 6, I will explain why it's important for you to have a starter emergency fund in place before tackling your debt. Let us now briefly discuss one category in particular from my budget I've been asked about during this journey – giving.

Should You Give/Tithe While In Debt?

In the survival budget example I discussed earlier, you may have noticed I included a category for giving. Giving can come in many different forms, such as giving monetarily, giving of one's time, and also giving of your talents and resources. For the purposes of this book, I will discuss giving as it pertains to money. The idea of giving while in debt or giving while trying to build wealth goes against the grain. It seems to defy common sense and logic. Why would you give while trying to get ahead financially? While many may think being stingy and holding on to everything you have is the fastest way to getting out of debt and building wealth, the exact opposite happens. Contrary to popular belief, there's a paradox that exists when it comes to giving; people who are generous tend to end up with more! Our household is all about giving and that's primarily because of our faith. Let me explain briefly.

Giving monetarily in the Bible is often referred to as a tithe. Simply put, the definition of a tithe is a percentage (*tithe* means a tenth or 10%) of your income that is given for support of the local church (anything beyond the tithe is considered an offering and it should not replace the tithe). One question Faith and I have been asked along our journey is whether or not you should tithe while in debt. The answer is yes. Giving is a biblical principle and mandate given to believers in the Bible. For this reason, I encourage folks to *tithe even while in debt and to give generously above their tithes once they are debt free.*

For us, giving is one way we say we trust God with our finances. As you can see, it clearly didn't stop us from paying off over $104,000 of debt! Plus, if you can't survive and do well off of 90% of your income then you have a much bigger issue that needs to be addressed. Here are a few reasons why Faith and I tithe:

- It is a mandate given to us by God.

- It shows that God has first place in our lives.

- It reminds us that everything we have belongs to God, including our money.

- It's a way to express gratitude and thankfulness for being able to earn income.

- Giving takes the focus off of us and opens our eyes to the needs of others.

Even non-believers understand the value of giving and being generous. Wealthy people, in general, are some of the most charitable individuals and will tell you giving is an essential part of their lives. Some would even say it's directly tied to their wealth!

Here are a few quotes on the benefit of giving by some well-known individuals:

- "No one has ever become poor by giving." - Anne Frank

- "I have found that among its other benefits, giving liberates the soul of the giver." - Maya Angelou

- "Only by giving are you able to receive more than you already have." - Jim Rohn

- "Giving is the master key to success, in all applications of human life." - Bryant McGill

Even birthday gifts, baby shower gifts, or wedding gifts can fall under the agreed upon giving budget. However, the desire to give and bless others does not give you the green light to be unwise with your finances. Once that giving budget is capped, wait until the following month's budget to continue in your giving. Regardless of your beliefs, I hope you'll discover the beauty of the timeless principle that it is better to give than to receive. You will be amazed to see just how liberating being generous can be.

Faith and I tithe 10% of all of our earned income to our local church. Because one of the visions for our family is to be a family that gives, we also have a giving fund above our tithing (the Jean-Louis Foundation) where we set a very small amount aside each month to give to different causes/people throughout the year. We hope to increase this amount once we're debt free and also hope to include our (future) children in the tradition of demonstrating random acts of kindness!

Your budget can be as comprehensive as you want it to be. Here are a few other options to consider when planning your budget.

Sinking Fund

Another category not listed above that is worthwhile to consider and can be useful on your journey to debt freedom is a sinking fund. A sinking fund is a category you can establish in your budget as a way to set aside money every month for a future big-ticket expense. Typically, when there is a need for a big-ticket expense, people tend to borrow money and go further into debt to get it. Having a sinking fund ensures you have a plan in place so you can be prepared for those expenses. Some examples of big-ticket expenses can include the purchase of a vehicle, saving up for a down payment on a home, or saving for a vacation. A sinking fund can also be used for ongoing car maintenance you will most likely have throughout the year and for car insurance premiums. To plan for car maintenance expenses, take a look at your records over the past year to see how much you spent on maintenance and allocate money every paycheck toward a sinking fund for it. You can do the same for car insurance premiums. By saving up for your car insurance premium throughout the year, you can take advantage of the discounts car insurance companies often offer for paying your policy in full when it comes time to renew.

If you NEED to purchase a vehicle while on your journey to debt freedom, I recommend you purchase your car cash. You must get out of the habit of financing things you do not yet have the money to purchase. Can you believe it's possible to purchase a car with 100% cash? Many people are going against the norm to save up for a car so they do not have to assume the burden of car payments, and you can too!

If your desire is to purchase a home, I highly recommend you wait until you are debt free. I know, rent prices are high and steadily increasing and you want to own your own home, but, as mentioned before, timing is essential. Owning a home is a very admirable and healthy goal. I want you to own your home, trust me, but not while you're over your head in debt. There are many added expenses that come with buying a home that are not your responsibility as a renter. This is your season to take advantage of that. As a renter, if your tub suddenly starts having trouble draining or your hot water heater stops working, you can easily call your apartment complex and have them fix it at no additional cost to you. However, as a homeowner, those costs would be passed down to you. Believe me, there will be so many expenses you did not foresee. One of our loans was a new HVAC unit I had to replace eight months after moving into my home. Not to mention, you will have more rooms to fill with furniture as your home will likely be bigger than the apartment you are currently renting. Moreover, your electric and gas bills will be higher. Even if your expected mortgage payment is the same or less than your current month's rent, it is not an "apples to apples" comparison. You will have soft costs such as property taxes, homeowner's insurance, and association fees to account for that will not always show up on an online mortgage calculator. Had I known what I know now, I would have delayed purchasing a home myself. Every potential expense you can eliminate will help propel you further on your journey to debt freedom. Once you are debt free, you can establish a sinking fund to save at least a 20% down payment for the purchase of a home, thereby eliminating private mortgage insurance (PMI). As stated in the sample zero-based budget above, when that time comes, your mortgage payment should not be more than 25-28% of your monthly take-home pay on a 15-year mortgage.

The Cash Envelope System

Figure 2.

The cash envelope system is yet another system you can implement when establishing your budget. This system is particularly helpful for those who have a hard time being disciplined with their budget and for those who tend to swipe their cards rather loosely. In this system, you would use separate envelopes to store money from each category in your budget. Those categories include giving, food, transportation, personal care/clothing, miscellaneous, etc. The amount of money you will need to withdraw in cash for each envelope is determined by the budget you set at the beginning of each month. Using the cash envelope system is a great way to make sure you do not go over budget because once you use all of the cash in an envelope, there is no more money left to spend in that category! Once the cash is spent in a specific category, we highly recommend not replenishing that envelope with money from other envelopes. Additionally, we do not recommend you carry every envelope with you at all times. Plan your week accordingly and only bring with you the envelope you intend to use that day. For example, if you normally go grocery shopping on Saturdays, only bring your grocery envelope with you that day. To prevent overspending on groceries, determine how often you go grocery shopping in a month. For example, if you go grocery shopping every Saturday and there are typically four Saturdays in a month, you would divide your total grocery budget by four and only carry with you the cash you need for that week's groceries. There is a huge psychological component to using the cash envelope system. People tend to spend less when they physically have to hand over cash versus swiping a card. Another trick is to use larger bills like $50 bills and $100 bills in your cash envelopes. You might be less likely to break that $50 bill for a $3 cup of coffee at Starbucks.

Multiple Bank Accounts

Some people decide to create multiple bank accounts as a way to keep track of the different categories in their budget. Having separate accounts can make it easier for you to see and manage your money and ultimately help you stick to your budget. Online savings accounts make it easy to do that. Think of this strategy as an online envelope system! This is a matter of preference vs. a requirement/recommendation. This is how it would work. Your direct deposit or paycheck would be deposited into your primary checking account; your primary checking account is the account from which your primary monthly bills such as rent, or utilities would be debited. You would then outsource funds from your primary checking account to the other accounts you created. The additional accounts can be used for categories such as non-monthly bills, your sinking fund, miscellaneous, emergency fund, etc.

INSIDE SCOOP

In addition to our primary checking and savings account, Faith and I have an online savings account for home maintenance, car maintenance, baby fund, the Jean-Louis Foundation (our giving fund), and estimated taxes.

Writing your budget on a single sheet of paper or in a notebook/journal is the way I would recommend you start your budget. You can also create your budget on an excel sheet if you so choose. Thanks to technology there are other resources available in the form of budgeting apps that will make your life much easier! Here are a few that come highly recommended.

Budgeting Apps

Mint.com

Mint is a free, web-based personal financial management service. It offers multiple services, including a budgeting app you can easily download on your smartphone, tablet, or another electronic device. Mint connects to almost every US financial institution connected to the internet and allows for you to link accounts, cards, and bills to their app. With this app, you have the opportunity to see everything in one place. You can create a budget using their pre-set categories or create your own based on the list I recommended above. It's important to make sure the categories you create cover every single expense type that your card will be used for so that nothing falls through the cracks.

EveryDollar Easy Budgeting App

The EveryDollar Budgeting App is a fun and easy to use budget planner and expense tracker. It is Dave Ramsey's own budgeting tool that follows the zero-based budget approach mentioned earlier in this chapter. This app offers you a simple, personalized way to give every dollar you earn a name, every month. It's free, compatible with iPhone, Android, or other electronic devices, and syncs across devices, making it easy to track expenses any time, any place. For those of you who are married, you and your spouse can access and update the same EveryDollar budget! My wife and I personally use this app. We input every expense on the app manually on the free version. Inputting every expense manually on the app really makes you aware of your spending and forces you to face your finances head on. There is a premium version to this app called EveryDollar Plus where you can link your cards and accounts, however, that version is $99/year at the time this book was written. If you're in debt, we recommend you utilize the free version.

YNAB (You Need A Budget)

YNAB is a multi-platform personal budgeting program based on the envelope system. Its software is compatible with Windows, Mac, iOS, and Android. YNAB offers bank synching, on the go real-time access to your info at any time, goal tracking, debt-payoff tools, and fun to read graphs and pie-charts. What sets YNAB apart is its large community of devout users who freely share tips on the app and the many support resources regarding finances that are available to the public from their home site. The company offers a 34-day free trial period which converts to $6.99/month, billed annually at $83.99 (at the time this book was written). Even more, YNAB offers all students the app for free for 12 months in addition to the free 34-day free trial!

Monthly Budget Meetings

A goal without a plan is just a wish.
-Antoine de Saint Exupéry

Establishing your budget can be a boring task. It's usually not the first thing people look forward to doing. We highly recommend you be proactive in this process instead of reactive by scheduling and planning monthly budget meetings ahead of time. Make sure everyone who is involved in your household spending (including your children) are a part of this meeting. That means you should not leave it up to one person to determine the budget. Your spouse should be involved every step of the way. That's why it's important to make sure you two are on the same page from the very beginning. Make your monthly budget meeting fun! My wife and I schedule our monthly budget meetings the last week and a half before the month we need to budget for. We have learned that starting relatively early gives us adequate time to discuss all of the things we need or want to do/purchase the following month. We also take that time to discuss how the current month is going and whether or not we need to make any adjustments to make sure we are within budget by month's end. To make it fun, we usually have our budget meetings over Chinese food or a 2-3 topping pizza from Domino's. You can be as creative as you want with your budget meetings. Have a mini ice cream party, pop some homemade popcorn, or have your meeting at the park. If you have children, include them in the process! Have your budget meeting in a play tent and ask for their opinions on some meals they would like or activities they would like to participate in the following month. It's important for them to get involved at a young age as this will be a great way for you to start teaching them about financial literacy. Budgeting takes the guilt out of spending – it is you giving yourself permission to spend but with boundaries. This is an exciting time as you can be assured you will finally be successful with your money going forward.

It is important to note that there will be a learning curve when you start budgeting; trial and error, if you will. I can guarantee that you will experience some hiccups in the beginning. Those chances increase even more if you are starting a budget as a newlywed couple learning to combine the lifestyle and finances of two individuals. It will likely take you 2-3 months to really buckle down on your line items and get your budget to the point where nothing is falling through the cracks. By now, I hope you've learned why budgeting is such an integral step on your journey to debt freedom.

- Budgeting provides you with a way to track your spending.

- Budgeting gives you the opportunity to tell your money where to go before you receive your paycheck or direct deposit for the month.

- Having a budget and sticking to it helps reduce the stress and worry regarding finances and removes the uncertainty of not knowing where your money is going. Isn't the formula for budgeting easy to remember? Earn an income, prioritize by telling your money where it goes, and stick to your plan. It's that easy!

I believe one of the lessons you will find most surprising when you start budgeting is just how much you can actually do with what you have now that you are learning to master the art of budgeting. So, control your finances – don't let your finances control you.

ACTIVITY: TRACK YOUR SPENDING

1. Look at your expenses over the past 1-3 months.
2. Print/download your bank statements and credit card statements for that time frame.
3. For each month, write EVERY expense down and place them under specific budget categories (housing, utilities, transportation, food, clothing, etc.).
4. THEN, ask yourself the following questions.
   a. Did you find anything surprising/alarming after tracking your spending? If so, what did you find?
   b. In what areas are you doing well in?
   c. In what areas are you overspending?
5. Adjust your budget as necessary.

Critical Thinking Questions

1. Why is it important to have a plan for your finances?

2. We all have weak moments where we *break* the budget because *life happens*. What are several tools that can help you stay the course while on a budget?

The BULLETPROOF Steps in Review

STEP 1: DREAM

Establish your reason(s) for wanting to be debt free. This is the *why* behind the *what*. Your DREAM is the reason you start your journey, the reason you do not quit, the reason your spouse gets on board, and so much more! This is the first step toward debt freedom.

STEP 2: KNOW HOW MUCH YOU OWE

Identify your target number. This is your debt-free goal amount. List all of the lending institutions you owe, along with the current balance and interest rates for each loan. You cannot effectively strategize unless you know the exact amount you're up against.

STEP 3: BUDGET

Create a plan for your money. Give each dollar you earn an *assignment* before you ever receive your paycheck.

This way all of your money is accounted for and not one penny is falling through the cracks. The formula is simple: Earn an income, prioritize by telling your money where it goes, and stick to your plan.

Chapter 6

STEP 4: STARTER EMERGENCY FUND

Build Your Walls – Protect Your City

So, I arrived in Jerusalem. Three days later, I slipped out during the night, taking only a few others with me. I had not told anyone about the plans God had put in my heart for Jerusalem. We took no pack animals with us except the donkey I was riding. After dark I went out through the Valley Gate, past the Jackal's Well, and over to the Dung Gate to inspect the broken walls and burned gates. Then I went to the Fountain Gate and to the King's Pool, but my donkey couldn't get through the rubble. So, though it was still dark, I went up the Kidron Valley instead, inspecting the wall before I turned back and entered again at the Valley Gate.

The city officials did not know I had been out there or what I was doing, for I had not yet said anything to anyone about my plans. I had not yet spoken to the Jewish leaders—the priests, the nobles, the officials, or anyone else in the administration. But now I said to them, "You know very well what trouble we are in. Jerusalem lies in ruins, and its gates have been destroyed by fire. Let us rebuild the wall of Jerusalem and end this disgrace!" Then I told them about how the gracious hand of God had been on me, and about my conversation with the king.

They replied at once, "Yes, let's rebuild the wall!" So, they began the good work.
- Nehemiah 2:11-18 NLT

THE OLDER I BECOME, the more responsibility I assume. The more responsibility I take on, the more I realize how likely and how quickly an emergency can happen. Such was not the case when I was younger. It's not because emergencies did not exist until I became an adult; it's that emergencies were taken care of by parents and elders, leaving me completely oblivious to a world with such a possibility. I have experienced several emergencies since becoming an adult and let me tell you, they are not fun, and they are even worse when you're not prepared financially. Don't you hate when you're doing your best to make better decisions and get ahead in life and something unexpected happens, such as car trouble or a leak in your home? And, it seems that with every step forward, you take two steps backward and can never catch a break? I have learned the hard way why it's important to have a starter emergency fund in place, especially before tackling your debt. I've included it in the steps so you can be prepared for the inevitable emergencies on your journey to debt freedom. Here's why.

An emergency is an unexpected life event that requires immediate action. It comes in varying degrees and it can be as serious as life or death or one that has the potential to cause harmful results if left unaddressed. No one likes emergencies. At least, I've never met or heard of anyone who does. They tend to occur at the most inconvenient times, are usually costly, and can put a damper on the best of days. Emergencies interfere with life and they will interfere with your plan to pay off your debt if you're not prepared. The sad reality is that most Americans are not prepared for an unplanned expense in the event of an emergency. According to the Federal Reserve's *Report on the Economic Well-Being of U.S. Households in 2017*, 40% of Americans would not be able to cover an unexpected expense of $400 without selling something or borrowing money.[1]

A 2015 survey conducted by GoBankingRates.com revealed that 62% of Americans had less than $1,000 saved in the event of an emergency. They conducted a follow-up survey in 2016 and found that the number of Americans with less than $1,000 in savings grew to 69%! What was even more alarming in those consecutive surveys was the percentage of people who had not even saved one penny. The number grew from 28% in 2015 to 34% in 2016![2]

What do you think is likely to happen when an

emergency situation that requires immediate action produces an unplanned expense? Are you equipped to withstand that? In such circumstances, people typically get into more debt by either using credit cards/loans to finance the expense, borrowing the money from a friend/relative, or compromising their budget (usually the debt category) in order to survive the blow. This series of events undoubtedly slows down your debt payoff goals or can completely derail you off track, leaving you discouraged and frustrated. Sadly, most people are one misfortune away from a financial disaster. Why ⅓ of Americans fail to save anything for an emergency is unfathomable. If you live long enough, you will realize that emergencies are a guaranteed part of life. Just ask Murphy.

Murphy's Law

Murphy's law is a popular old saying that states "anything that can go wrong will go wrong." Some versions of the saying even add "at the worst possible time" to the end of it. Does this not describe exactly how you feel after every emergency you've experienced? It seems that just as things are going well and you're getting your life in order, Murphy rears its ugly head without warning to get you off course. As I stated earlier in the chapter, emergencies come in varying degrees. It can be as serious or dangerous as a car accident, a medical emergency from a stroke, and a break in at your home or car, or as small as an unexpected injury during recreational sports that requires co-pays for doctors' visits and subsequent physical/occupational therapy services.

A few years before I started my debt-free journey, I purchased a home. Approximately eight months after closing on the house, my heating, ventilation, and air conditioning (HVAC) unit stopped working. You're probably thinking I should have hired a better inspector. Not only did I hire a home inspector, but I also hired an HVAC technician to inspect the unit because it was found to be leaking freon during the home inspection. We requested the repairs in our contract, which included the replacement of the evaporator coil, adding freon, and installation of new insulation for the rear HVAC unit coolant pipe. We received the receipts that all repairs were completed. The unit was in working condition when I moved in, but it still went out eight months later. After all the costs associated with purchasing a home, my funds were depleted, and I certainly did not have an emergency fund at the time. The end result was a financed HVAC unit in the amount of $6,311.48 on a newly opened Wells Fargo credit card. The remaining balance on the HVAC unit when I got married was $5,386, which contributed to the $200,000+ combined debt we had.

What about the time I locked my car and house keys inside the house on a weekday morning when I had to go to work? The end result was a $125 cost for a locksmith and an angry wife who was waiting for me to pick her up from her overnight side hustle shift. Or, what about the time when two of my car tires (which I purchased only two years prior) suddenly got nails in them conveniently around the same time I had to get front brakes and replace the rotors in my car? The end result was $723 to the automotive service center. You would think it couldn't get worse. It did. Two months later my wife's car battery stopped working and her brakes started randomly squeaking, requiring an additional expense totaling over $500. There was also the time my wife had to go to urgent care for a cost of $100 from what turned out to be strep throat. I think you get the point by now. I'm sure you've had your own personal experiences with Murphy. The reality is that he will be knocking on your door again, at the worst possible time. However, you don't have to be caught off guard financially.

Establishing Your $1,000 Emergency Fund

Before tackling your debt, I strongly recommend establishing an emergency fund of $1,000. This amount is certainly not much by any means, but it should cover most typical emergencies that could occur. This is not the fully funded emergency fund of 3-6 months or 6-9 months that you hear many financial experts recommend. That will be your goal once you are debt free. This is simply a *starter* emergency fund that serves as a buffer as you diligently try to pay off your debt. I know some people who believe a $1,000 emergency fund is not enough and are not comfortable having 'so little' cushion set aside. Those sentiments are very understandable. Here is one question to ask yourself if you're struggling with this recommendation. Think back to each emergency situation that occurred in your life over the past year. How many of them eclipsed the $1,000 mark? The answer to this question should help ease some of your concerns.

Establishing a $1,000 emergency fund while on your journey should help you remain on track with your debt payoff goals and, more importantly, help you avoid getting further into debt. This buffer emergency fund is not to be used for planned expenses like a car or a house. That's what your sinking fund is for. This fund gives you a cushion and a peace of mind for life's unexpected events. It is a safety net and a safeguard against your planned budget. You can store your $1,000 emergency fund in an online savings account in liquid form where it's easy to access in the event of an emergency. However, we recommend you store it in an online savings account that is separate from your primary checking account; you will be less likely to tap into it for non-emergencies if you don't see it every time you log in to your checking account. You should aim to open a high-yield online savings account, but don't become strung on that component. The main goal is to set up a wall of defense and security for your debt-free goal – not to earn money on it. When you do use some of your emergency fund, it is important for you to replenish it back to the recommended $1,000 amount as soon as possible. If your emergency happens to cost over $1,000, simply pay the minimum payment on your debt for that month and allocate any extra monies toward the emergency so you can get back on your feet. Emergencies are inevitable. Be proactive about your goal to eliminate your debt by first setting up a great defensive plan in the form of a $1,000 emergency fund. You'll be glad you did.

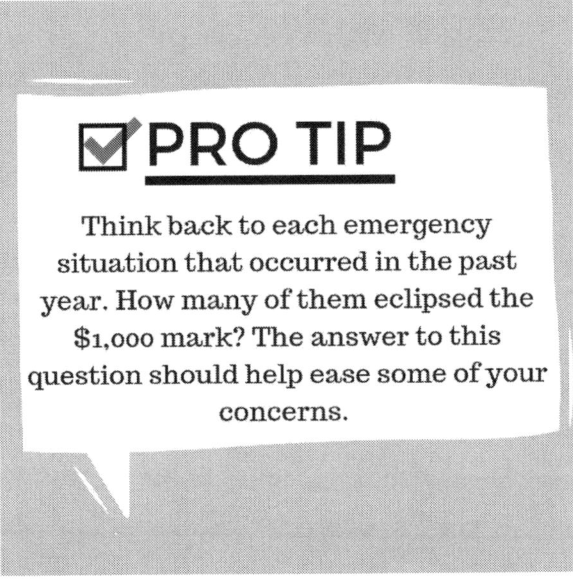

Special circumstances: The $1,000 recommendation is a general rule and, while it can work for most people, it may not work for everyone. This may be the case for those who live in states like California and New York where the cost of living is much higher than others. In those states, $1,000 might not go as far. For individuals who are in this situation, I recommend saving *one month's rent and utilities* as a *starter emergency fund.* The same recommendation would apply to those who have irregular incomes. For individuals with irregular incomes, a good question to ask yourself is how stable you feel at your current job. Again, looking back at the pattern over the past year will be a good indicator of how much you should set aside for a starter emergency fund. Generally speaking, anything beyond one month's rent and utilities may be excessive while on your journey to debt freedom. Do not fall for the trap to save more than you need to for your starter emergency fund; it is only a starter emergency fund that serves as a safeguard while you aggressively pay off your debt. If you are still fearful that this number is not enough, look back over the past year to track how many of your emergencies actually eclipsed that mark.

Critical Thinking Questions

1. In what ways is having a $1,000 emergency fund before tackling your debt similar to the idea of building the city walls to protect the city? Please reference the passage from Nehemiah 2:11-18 that was mentioned at the beginning of this chapter.

2. If you had an emergency situation today that cost you $1,000, would you be able to pay for it in cash or would you have to go further into debt to cover the expense?

The BULLETPROOF Steps in Review

STEP 1: DREAM

Establish your reason(s) for wanting to be debt free. This is the *why* behind the *what*. Your DREAM is the reason you start your journey, the reason you do not quit, the reason your spouse gets on board, and so much more! This is the first step toward debt freedom.

STEP 2: KNOW HOW MUCH YOU OWE

Identify your target number. This is your debt-free goal amount. List all of the lending institutions you owe, along with the current balance and interest rates for each loan. You cannot effectively strategize unless you know the exact amount you're up against.

STEP 3: BUDGET

Create a plan for your money. Give each dollar you earn an *assignment* before you ever receive your paycheck. This way, all of your money is accounted for and not one penny is falling through the cracks. The formula is simple: Earn an income, prioritize by telling your money where it goes, and stick to your plan.

STEP 4: STARTER EMERGENCY FUND

Establish a starter emergency fund as a layer of protection and buffer against life's unexpected events as you diligently execute a plan to pay off your debt. This will ensure you remain on track on your journey and do not get further into debt. Emergencies will happen, but you do not have to be unprepared.

Chapter 7

STEP 5: DECREASE EXPENSES + INCREASE INCOME

Two Sides of The Equation

> **_Counterforce_** – A strategy used in nuclear warfare of targeting military infrastructure (as opposed to civilian targets).
>
> **_Countervalue_** – The opposite of counterforce; targeting of enemy assets such as cities and civilian populations as a way to threaten the enemy.

YOU ARE NOW OVER HALFWAY THROUGH the steps of becoming free from consumer debt! BULLETPROOF STEP 5 is to decrease your expenses and increase your income. This is a two-part step that will help you maximize your potential to pay off your debt faster than expected! I am positive you have heard people recommend decreasing your expenses if you want to be debt free. This is a practical step most people understand but find it difficult to implement because doing so requires a change in behavior and lifestyle that they are just not quite ready, comfortable, or willing to do. You have probably also heard it recommended to increase your income by working extra hours or picking up an extra job. This is also a practical step most people understand but find it difficult to act on for various reasons, including life circumstances (single mother with no one to babysit, for example), not knowing what kind of jobs to do, being too picky or lazy, etc. Some people choose to do one option or the other. I say you must do both. By doing both, you could potentially shave off years from your timeline to pay off your debt! Remember, the faster you pay your debt off, the less you pay in interest over the life of your loan and the less time you will spend being enslaved to it. I contend that unless both sides of the equation are at work in your plan, you will miss out on the opportunity to fast-track the process to debt elimination. Who wants to be in debt any longer than they have to when it is within their power to control it? By the end of this chapter, you will learn how you can begin to execute a plan that will accelerate your debt payoff goals by decreasing your expenses and increasing your income.

> *We go on multiplying our conveniences only to multiply our cares. We increase our possessions only to the enlargement of our anxieties.*
> - Anna C. Brackett

In Chapter 2, I introduced the issue of debt in America. I briefly discussed the potential dangers it poses and some of the consequences it can lead to if left unaddressed. While debt is a major problem in America and it would be difficult to find someone who is not affected by it, it is only a symptom. The source of the problem is actually our spending, or rather our mindset about spending, that then leads to the propensity to borrow. The reason many Americans live paycheck to paycheck is that they spend more than they make. What is going out of their pocket (expenses) is more than what is coming in (income). The consumerist society we live in feeds into that. "Keeping up with the Joneses" is the phrase made popular by the 1913 cartoon strip that poked fun at our need to do things in order to impress other people. There is this societal pressure on us to put on a certain persona and flaunt our successes. We purchase things we don't need and can't afford with money we do not have. We never think we have enough, and we aren't content with what we do have. We value instant gratification over hard work. We want the latest and greatest gadget, the bigger house, designer clothes, the fancier car, etc. People honestly believe having more stuff will make them happier. This is a fundamental issue. It's okay to have nice things, but don't allow nice things to have you. We fall into the trap of finding our identity in the things we own and fail to realize they are merely objects of future garage sales. The thrill and joy of having or buying something new is a fleeting one. It is the never-ending desire to fill our lives with things that will ultimately never fully satisfy. We are happy for a short time until the next new fad rolls around. It used to be that we were trying to keep up with the Joneses, now we're trying to keep up with the Kardashians.

The grass isn't always greener on the other side. Behind the luxury cars are families drowning in debt wondering how they're going to pay the next bill. Behind the closed doors of big houses are money fights. Behind the fancy clothes and designer shoes are discontent people. It's easy to look like you have more than you do. However, more will never be enough. The insatiable desire to accumulate more is why most people are in debt to begin with. You cannot expect to live like your parents are living within a few years of starting your career; it took them over 20 years to be where they are right now. Be patient. Your time will come.

Stop All Non-Essential Spending

As I stated earlier in the book, you don't become debt free by spending money and you definitely won't get out of debt if you continue to spend like you're used to. So, the first step toward decreasing your expenses is to stop all non-essential spending. Go on a *spending freeze* where you don't purchase or spend money on anything outside of your basic necessities. Try this for a month or you can start by doing this for two weeks if you need to start with baby steps. That means saying *no* to your wants. That's one of the most valuable lessons I've learned on my journey – the power of saying *no*. You don't need to go to that concert. You don't need to buy that gadget or eat out again. You have all you need. This would also be a great time to cancel any subscriptions and memberships you have not used in a while. That can include gym memberships, magazine subscriptions, etc. A good rule of thumb to use when you get that irresistible urge to buy something is to wait one full day before making a decision. You will be surprised to see how many times you snap out of it and realize you don't actually need to make that purchase.

Negotiate or Shop Around to Find Better Rates

Negotiating and shopping around to find better rates might be one of the easiest ways to decrease your expenses. For one, you can do it from the comfort of your home. Secondly, it requires nothing more than making a few phone calls or filling out some forms online. While implementing this strategy can potentially save you thousands over the course of the year, it is seldom used. Why? The reason is simple. People have become accustomed to paying the same monthly premiums, so unless there is a huge change to their bills, they do not think about it. Some individuals don't notice subtle increases in their bills when they do occur. I make it a point to negotiate and shop around at least once or twice a year for better rates on my services and, 9 out of 10 times, I am successful!

Our friend, Heather, saved a staggering $6,444 on car insurance earlier this year in just 10 minutes! She had been with her car insurance company for five years with no accidents when she noticed her car insurance bill increased. Puzzled by the change, she decided to shop around for better rates and boy did she find one. Just 10 minutes after initiating the call, she found the same coverage with another company for $6,444 cheaper (over the span of a few years) and canceled the policy she had!

Not only can you shop around for better rates, but you can also call your current providers to negotiate a lower bill. You can potentially even lower interest rates on your credit card(s) if there is evidence that your financial situation has improved. These strategies can be used for almost any bills you have, including the gas company for your home, cable/internet, car insurance, homeowner's/renter's insurance, etc. You will be surprised at how much you can save by implementing this simple hack!

Cut Up Your Credit Cards

Cut up your credit cards. If you use a credit card, you don't want to be rich. - Mark Cuban

Figure 1. Retrieved from https://wallethub.com/edu/canceling-unused-credit-cards-and-credit-scores/25563/ [1]

This suggestion might step on the toes of those who use credit cards as lifestyle hacks. These individuals swear by the use of credit cards to earn cash back rewards, travel rewards, or store rewards for ongoing discounts. The argument on this side of the debate is centered around the potential to earn free money on the things you would normally buy anyway. This argument is logical and the benefits are super enticing! Who wouldn't want free money? However, those who advocate for the use of credit cards for such hacks need to factor in this one very important fact – it would only work if individuals are responsible enough to pay their balances in full at the end of each month. Well, we all know this isn't the case. Most people who use credit cards carry a balance from month to month. The banks know this all too well. It's one of the many traps they set for us. Customers typically earn between 1% - 5% cash back on purchases while the bank earns north of 15% on average given the high likelihood that most customers will carry a balance into the following month. Who wins in that trade-off?

For those who pay off their balance every month, let's be honest, credit card rewards will not make you rich. The use of credit cards gives a false sense of security and can push you further into debt. It's not uncommon for individuals who use them to believe they aren't spending as much or to believe they have more than they actually do. Frictionless payments have further exacerbated the problem by increasing the ease at which people can spend money they don't really have. Think about it; it's much easier to swipe your card when you can't *feel* the spending. That's probably how you got into massive credit card debt to begin with. All it takes is one purchase here and another one there and, before you know it, you will find yourself slipping again. If you're serious about getting out of debt, then you need to stop the habitual spending on your credit cards. The first actionable step is grabbing a pair of heavy-duty scissors and cutting them up, immediately!

In BULLETPROOF STEP 3, you began your budget by tracking your spending. Now, let's take a look at some areas where you can begin to cut back.

Shelter (Housing)

Housing is one of the five basic necessities of life. You should not prioritize paying off your debt if you do not have a place to lay your head at night. That would not be wise. However, just because housing is a necessity, it doesn't give you the green light to live above your means in this area. Housing cost is likely the single most expensive line item in your budget. I recommend that your monthly housing (rent or mortgage payment) cost be 25-28% or less of your monthly take-home pay. To determine what percentage of your income is currently going toward housing expenses, you would take your monthly rent and divide it by the amount you earn in income for the month. If you have a mortgage, your monthly mortgage payment should be 25-28% or less of your monthly take-home pay as well, but on a 15-year mortgage – not a 30-year mortgage. Why would you want to be in debt for 30 years when you have the ability to choose otherwise? You will pay much more in interest on a 30-year loan by holding on to a mortgage for that long! Take a look at the illustration below to see how much you can save by choosing a 15-year mortgage over a 30-year mortgage.

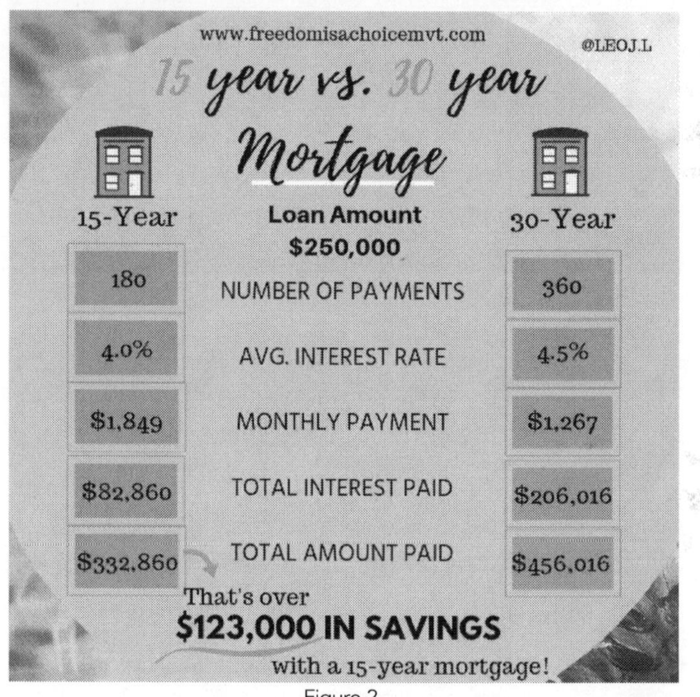

Figure 2.

If you are currently on a 30-year mortgage, plug in the current balance of your home on an online mortgage calculator with your respective interest rate to determine what your monthly payment would be on a 15-year mortgage. If the monthly mortgage payment would be more than 25-28% of your monthly take-home pay on a 15-year mortgage, then you have too much house. This means that too much of your income will be going to this category and will consequently put an unnecessary strain on the rest of your budget. After all, a bigger house or larger/more luxurious apartment simply means you will need more furniture, have a higher electric bill, higher water bill, more potential repairs, increased lawn care, etc.

For example, I know someone in debt who is struggling to keep their head above water with their finances but has a mortgage payment of $1,000 while bringing home $3,000/month. That's over 33% of their budget taken up by a mortgage payment! And, it's on a 30-year mortgage. There is no wonder this person is struggling financially. They are house poor! I spoke to another individual who overheard me speaking to a group about budgets and the percentages to allocate per category. This young lady had no idea how much of her take-home pay, percentage-wise, was going toward her mortgage. Intrigued by what I was saying, she pulled out her phone to access the calculator. After crunching the numbers, my jaw dropped. Her mortgage payment was 50% of her take-home pay! Can you believe that? Half of her income was being used to pay for one category in her budget and that number did not even include utilities! That only left her with 50% to pay for all of her other needs. Do you see the problem with this scenario? The crazy part about all of this is that she had no idea! I'm sure there are many people just like her who are unaware that their house/apartment is more of a curse than a blessing. If you have a *house problem*, you can solve it by either increasing your income so that your monthly payment falls within the recommended 25-28% or downsizing to a home that fits in that range. Consider house hacking by rooming together with a few friends to reduce your housing cost or consider renting out a room in your home. It is understandable for you to be attached to your place of residence, but it is not wise to continue living in a place that is costing you your freedom.

INSIDE SCOOP 

Our total housing costs, including paying off our mortgage as if it were a 15-year loan, and all utilities for the home (electric, gas, HOA, garbage/sewer, etc.) is 18% of our budget.

Transportation

The car you drive is another area you may be spending too much on. This is a common area people tend to try to impress others in. They view cars as status symbols that indicate a social class/position and merit societal recognition. As a result, they finance vehicles that are often too expensive and choke the life out of their finances. According to the credit reporting agency Experian, the average monthly payment is $372 on a used vehicle and $523 on a new vehicle. That's $4,464-$6,276 per year on car payments alone! That does not include car insurance, gas, and routine maintenance, like oil changes. Here's a good rule of thumb to follow. The value of all of your vehicles should not exceed **35% of your annual income**. If you earn 50,000, you should not be driving a $30,000 car. Say that out loud. You make $50,000/year and your car is worth $30,000. Doesn't that sound beyond ridiculous? Did you know that a new car loses 10% of its value as soon as you drive it off the lot and it loses another 10% within the first year? What's even more eye-opening is that on average, a new car will lose 60% of its total value over the first five years of its life.[2] How can you ever recoup those costs?

If you are in need of a vehicle, I highly recommend you save to pay cash for a used car. Yes, pay cash! It's totally possible. You don't need anything fancy. Your car should be reliable and meet all of your functional needs. This may not bode well with many. In their minds, saving to pay cash for a car would take too long and would require too much sacrifice. However, don't fall victim to the pressure to purchase more than you can afford. One reason people finance cars is that the price of the vehicle is too high. Nowadays, many of the auto loans are being lengthened to six or seven years in an attempt to make the payments seem "affordable" for you. What car buyers don't realize is that they are still paying a really high price for the car and that the lengthening of the loan term will only cost them more in interest payments. Not to mention, they would be enslaved longer. Don't let that be you. Contrary to popular belief, you can find a reliable used car for $5,000-$7,500.

If you do own a car that is more than 35% of your annual income, you should consider selling it immediately and search for a car that falls within the recommended limits. Our friend, April, did just that by selling her beloved 2016 Audi Q5. At the time she made this daunting decision, she owed $33,700 to the Volkswagen creditors while her vehicle was only worth $27,500. Due to the depreciation of her car overtime, she was upside down $6,200 on her car and needed to come up with that amount in cash in order to be completely free of that debt. If you're upside down on your vehicle, come up with a plan to save up for the difference that you will owe the creditors in order to transfer the title of your vehicle to the new owner. After selling her car, April then rode the bus to work for a few months until she was able to save and pay cash for a more reasonably priced car that wouldn't continue to add to her burden of debt. What was formerly a $640.32 monthly car note and a $298/month car insurance payment turned into $938.32 of extra payments toward her monthly debt! Now that's a decision to decrease expenses that will undoubtedly help you pay off your debt faster!

INSIDE SCOOP

On the days Faith and I work on the same side of town, we carpool to work to decrease our expenses. This saves us approximately $2,000/year in gas/car maintenance costs.

Other options include riding a bike to work if you live close enough to your workplace or taking the bus/train.

Food

"The best part of waking up is…" Were you able to finish that sentence? Although most people know this popular jingle by Folgers coffee, it hasn't deterred coffee lovers from frequenting their favorite local coffee shops on their way to work in the mornings. The truth is, food is one category people tend to spend heedlessly on. A big reason for this is the convenience and ease at which people can satisfy their taste buds and cravings. Restaurants fill a need for individuals across the spectrum, including those who are too lazy to make their meals at home, those whose time is limited by busy work schedules, and those who enjoy socializing with their family/friends over a meal that required nothing more than for them to show up and order. Eating out reduces the time required to go grocery shopping and eliminates the time needed to learn how to cook. The time required to perform meal preparation or the task of cooking itself is decreased or completely removed. When people eat out, they also don't have to worry about washing dishes. Regardless of your reason for eating out on a regular basis, there is a goldmine of an opportunity to decrease a huge percentage of your spending in your food category if you can muster up the will to sacrifice convenience for what is more economical. Let's take a look at some practical changes you can make immediately in the food category.

INSIDE SCOOP

Entertainment and socialization are often associated with food-related expenses. Rather than spending a ton of money eating out all the time, we have potluck style gatherings with our friends. Each married couple takes turns hosting the gathering on a weekend that is usually filled with laughs, games, and great food.

Coffee

According to The National Coffee Association and The Specialty Coffee Association of America, over 50% of Americans over 18 years of age drink coffee every day. Among coffee drinkers, the average consumption in the United States is 3.2 cups of coffee per day.[3] Let's use Starbucks' most sold coffee product in the United States, freshly brewed coffee, to calculate what the average coffee drinker would spend throughout the month for their caffeine fix. The Grande (medium-size 16 oz. cup) of freshly brewed coffee at Starbucks is $2.25 (hot) and $3.45 (cold) before taxes in the Metro-Atlanta area. In this example, I will be conservative and calculate the numbers based on two cups per day rather than three cups. If a loyal Starbucks customer consumed freshly brewed hot coffee twice a day, every day during the work week, the total amount spent would be $22.50 for the week and $90 for the month before taxes. See the breakdown below:

$2.25 x 2 cups per day = $4.50
$4.50 x 5 days per week = $22.50
$22.50 x 4 weeks in a month = $90

Keep in mind that this does not include any coffee purchases on the weekends or that third cup of coffee reported in the statistics.

Did you know that a 48 oz. canister of Folgers Classic Roast Ground Coffee holds enough ground coffee to make 380 six-ounce cups and only costs $11.68 (before taxes) at Walmart? That is the equivalent of 126 eighteen-ounce cups! Divide that number by two cups per day and the coffee you bought for $11.68 (before taxes) at Walmart would last you 63 days! Compare that to the $90 it would cost you to get two cups of coffee Monday-Friday for four weeks (20 days) at Starbucks. You probably don't even realize how much those small purchases are costing you over time. You would be surprised to see how much you can save by deciding to brew your own coffee at home.

Starbucks Freshly Brewed Coffee	Folgers Classic Roast Ground Coffee (48 oz. Canister)
Two 16 oz. Cups per day	Two 18 oz. Cups per day
$22.50/week (5-day work week) or $90/month	$11.68 for two months
20-day supply	63-day supply

Table 1.

Packing Lunches

Lunchtime is yet another missed opportunity for people to decrease their expenses. Rather than packing lunches, many employees head to their local cafeteria or to a nearby restaurant to grab lunch with their co-workers. The socialization component here is a huge factor. Who wants to be the only person at the office with a lunch box packed with a ham sandwich and BBQ Pringles while everyone else around them has tasty takeout meals? I know that feeling of awkwardness and shamefulness all too well. It took me some time to overcome the pressure of feeling like I had to buy lunch just because others were. When I looked at the numbers, the decision became easier. Conservatively, people spend at least $7-$10 per lunch meal depending on where they eat (this is a very conservative number). Multiply that by 5 days/week and what you have is $35-$50/week and $140-$200/month spent on lunch alone! You can spend half of that amount per month on lunches for two people by deciding to pack your own lunch for work every day.

INSIDE SCOOP

Faith and I pack our lunches to work every day. Faith has even influenced some of her co-workers who eat out for lunch to start bringing their own lunches to work. I smiled one day when I saw one of her co-workers leaving the job with a lunch box as I was picking Faith up from work in the afternoon. By bringing our lunches to work EVERY day, we save approximately $3,000/year!

Dinner Time

Lunch hour is not the only time of the day restaurants are booming with crowds coming in to order meals. The busiest time of the day for restaurants, aside from the weekends, are the evenings when most individuals are often too tired to want to cook. It is no surprise that dining out during dinner time is even more costly than grabbing something to eat for lunch. It is a given that prices are higher for dinner. However, there is no need to bore you again with numbers showing you the amount of money you could save by choosing to cook your own meals. I believe by now you know this is an area that has been eating away at your budget. No pun intended! If you want to propel yourself into debt freedom at a much faster pace, it will require some sacrifice. I'm not telling you not to eat. I am simply suggesting you decrease your expenses by making your own meals at home. You can even learn to cook some of those same meals you love to order when you eat out. If you are recently married like my wife and I were when we started learning of ways to decrease our spending, turn meal prep and cooking into a fun activity you could do together! If you have children, get them involved too. Ask for their input on the meals for the week, have them help with any age-appropriate tasks, and bond over this experience while saving money. And, if you want to save even more, do your grocery shopping at Aldi!

We meal prep and cook dinner for the week to prevent us from eating out unnecessarily. It's much easier to fight the urge and stick to your plan when you have food already prepared at home.

Groceries

If you have an Aldi in your area and you have not stopped

by there to visit, you are missing out! Aldi is a supermarket retail chain selling a wide range of grocery items including produce, meat, and dairy at discounted prices. Making Aldi our primary grocery store was a total game changer for our budget! Their entire business model revolves around great quality at everyday low prices. When Faith and I started doing our grocery shopping there, we immediately noticed a huge reduction in the price we paid at checkout. There are several reasons for the inexpensive prices at this grocery store chain. They include the following: they avoid using name brands as much as possible by having their own exclusive brands; they offer a smaller selection of items (~900 core products) and the stores are smaller, resulting in lower rent costs; their store design was created for minimal stocking and upkeep, requiring less employees; customers bring their own bags and bag their items; there's a smart shopping cart rental system where you put a quarter in the cart in order to unlock it and use it (you get your coin back once you return the cart); and they use energy efficient lighting, further reducing their costs.

Doesn't this sound like a grocery store from heaven?

For those fortunate enough to have an Aldi located near you, what are you waiting for? For those without this option, here's a list of the 7 most affordable grocery stores in America according to a recent survey by Consumer Reports.[4]

1. Aldi

2. Costco

3. Fareway

4. Market Basket

5. Trader Joe's

6. WinCo.

7. Woodman's

Do a simple google search to see if any of these grocery stores have locations near you!

Below are some additional tips to consider that will help you decrease your expenses even more.

- Meal plan by thinking ahead of time what you would like to eat for breakfast, lunch, and dinner throughout the week. A lack of meal planning is most likely the culprit behind your overspending in the food category.

- Clean out your fridge and pantry to see what needs to be replenished.

- Write down a grocery list on your phone or with pen and paper. Having a grocery list helps you remain focused on what is needed and helps you avoid over-buying or forgetting items. It's very important to stick to the grocery list when you are grocery shopping.

- Look ahead at the sale items and base your food for the week off of what is on sale.

- Make sure you do not go grocery shopping on an empty stomach! You will definitely get an uncontrollable urge to spend more than you planned to.

INSIDE SCOOP 

After creating the grocery list for the week, Faith typically goes to Aldi first and whatever she does not find there, she usually gets at Walmart.

Couponing

Couponing is a great way to purchase items in bulk at a reduced price, saving you hundreds of dollars on things you would normally buy for your household. This life hack is not for everyone and will require time, planning, and organization in order to be successful. This is a not a way to get products for free but a way to get products (brand name products, too) at a discounted price. You can use online databases such as http://www.klip2save.com/ and www.southernsavers.com to order coupons or you can obtain them in person through newsletters or weekly ads from some of your favorite stores. Some online databases have coupons that have already been *clipped*, meaning the coupon has already been cut out for you or *unclipped*, meaning it comes in a sheet of paper from a newsletter or weekly ad that you will have to cut out yourself. If cutting and clipping isn't your thing, don't worry. Many stores have their own apps that allow you to access in-store deals digitally. Kroger and Target are two good examples. Additionally, southernsavers.com and Honey App have coupon deal apps that aggregate deals into one place and allow you to search which stores have the best prices.

Make sure to read the fine print on coupons. Mostly all of them will have some type of restriction. For example, a coupon might say "Buy One, Get One Free," "Limit one coupon per person or transaction," or "No more than four of these coupons per transaction." Find out your store's coupon policy on their website. Most stores have a cap on how many coupons you can use per transaction.

It is important to forego the temptation to purchase coupons just because a product is on sale. Only buy items that you know you will definitely use. Create your grocery shopping list like you would normally, and see which coupons match the items on your list. My cousin, Ketura, coupons mostly on cereal, pop tarts, milk, and Tyson chicken for food items and on toilet paper, paper towels, and detergent (non-food items) because she knows she is guaranteed to use these items throughout the year based on her family needs.

When couponing you must be organized in order to make the most efficient use of your time. Find a system that works for you. Use a binder to keep track of expiration dates and to track your savings results. A good suggestion is to start by purchasing 5-10 coupons at a time and/or to start by focusing on 1-2 products just so you can get a gist of how couponing works. Once you're comfortable, you can slowly ramp up and begin to stockpile your pantry.

It is worth mentioning that there are cashback apps that offer another quick and easy way to save money after you do your grocery shopping. Cashback apps like Ibiotta, Checkout 51, and SavingStar offer cash back options for shoppers who purchase specific items. If you are struggling to find room in your budget, this may be a great way to start decreasing your expenses for what some couponers say can be a 40-50% savings on your weekly grocery budget!

Cutting the Cord

If you still have cable TV, you might be living in the Stone Age! Say goodbye to the days of paying hundreds of dollars for channels you barely watch. Nowadays, there exist a plethora of reasonably priced online streaming options for those wishing for Cable TV alternatives at a substantially reduced price! Streaming services like Hulu, Netflix, Amazon Prime Video, YouTube TV and many others offer tons of shows, movies, and live television channels to meet your entire binge-watching needs. Some of them, like Sling TV, even offer tiered packages where you can personalize your television experience by customizing with add-ons like sports packages and kid's networks at additional costs. This option allows you to pay for channels you will actually watch instead of paying premium prices for a cable package consisting of channels you could care less about.

You can even wisely share the service with family or a close friend to distribute the cost while still getting all of your streaming needs met. For example, you can pay for the Netflix and Sling TV accounts while a friend or family member pays for the Hulu and Fubo TV accounts and share access with each other. You can also share one account by splitting up the annual payment between three people so that everyone can enjoy Hulu or Netflix for a lower cost. For example, for $15.99 per month, you can watch Hulu across three screens. This is a breakdown of how it would work:

- Multiply $15.99 by 12 to get your annual cost.
  - Your annual cost will be $191.88
- Divide the annual amount by the number of users to determine the annual cost per person. In this example, we will divide by three users.
  - $191.88 divided by 3 = $63.96
- Collect the annual payment from all users before you sign up for the account to avoid having to collect payments every month.
- You now have access to one streaming service for the entire year at a significantly reduced price!

Sharing services may not be allowed for all streaming services. Please read the fine print in your contract and/or call the company for further details.

Additionally, there are streaming devices like Roku,

Amazon Fire Stick, and Google Chromecast that give you access to free channels and movies. These streaming devices also allow you to add the applications of the streaming services mentioned above for a one-stop shop to stream all of your desired content to your television. These devices are a one-time cost. It is important to note that you will still need an internet service with all of these options. The streaming junkies haven't figured out a way around that yet! Are you ready to decrease your expenses by cutting the cord? Well, what are you waiting for?

INSIDE SCOOP

We use a TV antenna purchased from Walmart to access some local channels with the signal we are able to receive from the cell towers near our home. We are able to access ABC, NBC, FOX, CBS, ION Television and several other channels for free! We also own a Fire Stick and share access to Netflix and DirecTV accounts with close family members.

It is only by saying no that you can concentrate
on the things that are really important.
          – Steve Jobs

If you and your family are struggling to find wiggle room in your current budget, I hope that problem has now been solved. You now have no excuse as to what you can begin to do to decrease your expenses. Sure, it will require you to make some sacrifices by learning to say *no* to the things you want. I know this will not be easy for you, but you will succeed if you CHOOSE to commit. Your mind has been trained to swipe your credit card for years without thinking twice about it. However, you don't need to buy that designer purse or shoes. You're in debt! Louis Vuitton is going to do fine with or without you. Learn to tell yourself *no*. Learn to tell others *no*. The world is not going to end if you don't get that item right now. Remember that with every *yes* you say to the things you want but don't really need, you are simultaneously saying *no* to a debt-free financial future.

There is no way you can make a big dent in your debt payoff goals unless you create a way to generate more cash to allocate toward it. Decreasing your expenses by living below your means is one way to do that and the categories mentioned above are just some of the areas you can begin to make some changes in. However, if you closely monitor your spending, I'm sure you can find even more areas where you can cut back.

> *Cutting back has a limit. Your earning potential is limitless. - Jamila Souffrant*

Faith and I started fast-tracking our debt payoff goals by decreasing our expenses. When we sat down for our monthly budget meetings, we looked at each category in our budget for ways to decrease our spending. That's how we came up with reducing our food costs. We brought our own lunches to work and cooked dinner at home for the week instead of eating out all of the time. Each time we discussed our budget, we would look for even more ways to decrease our spending. Then came carpooling to work three days a week on the days when we worked on the same side of town, cutting the cord, and significantly limiting personal expenses. At some point during the process, there was only so much meat we could take off the bone! There was no longer any more room to cut back on expenditures short of starving ourselves and living in a shack! We had developed a really strict budget! It was then that we changed gears to focus more on the other side of the equation – increasing our income!

Ask for a Raise

You miss 100% of the shots you don't take.
-Wayne Gretzky

The easiest way you can increase your income is by asking for a raise. This may seem like a daunting and intimidating proposition, but do not let that stop you. Be prepared to justify your reason(s) for requesting the raise. Those reasons can include, but are not limited to, obtaining a new job-related certification, performance-based results, and a market correction for your position. Plan to initiate the conversation a few months before your yearly review and push for a raise rather than a bonus. While earning a bonus is good, a raise offers far greater value because it can pave the way for a higher salary in the future. Is the thought of approaching your employer increasing your anxiety? Do not allow it to. After all, what's the worst that could happen?

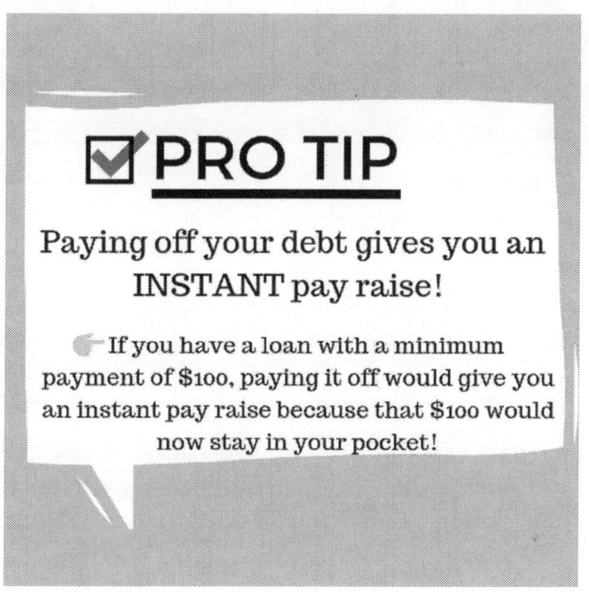

Avoid Lifestyle Creep

If you get a bonus or earn a raise from your job, the first thought that comes to mind is probably how you're going to spend that money. Maybe it's purchasing that new truck you had your eye on for a while or those pair of shoes you saw on the internet the other day. Lifestyle creep is the gradual increase in spending as wages increase. It's a slippery slope that can occur without you even noticing it. Things that were once luxuries all of a sudden become necessities. It is one of the major reasons people don't get ahead in life. They move into a fancier apartment. They get the membership to the gym just to realize they don't even attend regularly. They literally spend all of the money they earn without any concept of the future. If you're expecting an increase in income via a bonus or a raise, plan to continue to live below your means by spending less than you earn. Trust me, you will be just fine. Make a plan for the extra cash to get you out of debt first and once you're debt free, use that money to build wealth!

INSIDE SCOOP 

In 2018, I was fortunate enough to receive a 12.9% raise from my job. Guess what I did with it? I used all of that additional income to fast-track our debt payoff goals!

It Takes Two to Tango

If you have decreased your expenses by exhausting every budget cut possible within reason and still cannot find enough money to make significant extra payments toward your debt, then you now have an income problem. Increasing our income by working side jobs/side hustles has been the single most impactful and powerful accelerator of our debt payoff goals. It's a huge reason we were able to pay off $104,221.89 in just 12 months! As this book is being written, Faith and I have 5 jobs between the two of us, including our primary jobs as an occupational therapist and a pediatric nurse practitioner. For side hustles, Faith babysits for a family three days a week for a few hours per day. She also works as a night-time nurse for parents with newborn babies who desire to get a good night's rest so they can be productive during the day. For my side hustle, I work in my same field as an occupational therapist and pick up shifts at the local hospital on the weekends and most holidays. Because increasing our income has been so instrumental on our journey to debt freedom, we've decided to include it as part of BULLETPROOF STEP 5 and give you practical options you can explore to start working the income side of the equation.

Side Hustle/Job vs. Entrepreneurship

Side Hustle/Job

A side hustle (or a side job) is anything you do in addition to your full-time or part-time job to earn extra income. Side hustles come in varying forms and do not necessarily have to be something you enjoy doing. It is a means to an end. Having a side hustle places you in an employee-like position as it will generally require you to trade your time for money. However, unlike your primary job, you can choose to work as few or as many hours as you would like. And, there's no limit on how many side hustles you can have at a given time. The biggest benefit, of course, is that it allows you to supplement your income in order to accomplish specific goals at a much faster pace.

Entrepreneur

Being an entrepreneur is much different than having a side hustle. As an entrepreneur, you are the owner of a business (enterprise). The goal of an entrepreneur is to build a self-sustaining business that may reap huge rewards but at the same time involves risk and perhaps, a delayed return on investment. Entrepreneurs are able to free up their time by relying heavily on systems, automation, and employees that don't require their physical presence. This, in turn, allows them to ideally maximize their time by being able to delve into other business ventures and investments to generate more cash. Additionally, it affords them the flexibility to do the things they enjoy like spending time with family or participating in hobbies without being confined to a predetermined schedule.

Benefits of Both

There are some mutual benefits to having a side hustle and being an entrepreneur. Individuals who are self-employed, have side hustles, are contractors, and who are entrepreneurs can take tax deductions that W-2 employees cannot take. Some major examples include the following:

- Under the new tax law (2019 filing season), you may qualify to take a free 20% deduction on your income.
- Home office deduction if you are home-based.
- Mileage deduction on your car for trips related to your business.
- Deduction of equipment and materials you use to run your side hustle or business venture (laptop, phone, website costs, etc.).

Disclaimer: The information above is not offered as tax advice. Please be sure to seek the counsel of a tax professional first before making any changes and/or to gain more clarity on the subject matter.

Which is the Better Option?

Well, how do you make the correct choice between either pursuing side hustles or entrepreneurship? The answer for entrepreneurship can be summed up in the three P's coined by Michael Hyatt: Passion. Proficiency. Profitability. In order to become an entrepreneur, you must love what you do (Passion), be excellent and talented at it (Proficiency), and be able to earn a living with it (Profitability). Just because you love baking and are good at it, doesn't mean the market is willing to pay for what you offer. Here are some questions Michael Hyatt poses about each category.[5]

Regarding Passion: What do you love? What do you

love learning about?

Regarding Proficiency: What are you good at and what do your friends say you're good at? In what areas have you been rewarded or acknowledged?

Regarding Profitability: Can you make money doing this with a clear strategy to scale? Is there a market willing to pay for what you offer?

The intersection of these three ingredients must be present in order for you to be a successful entrepreneur. So, which is the better option? I encourage you to pursue entrepreneurship but only if you've identified a problem and are able to provide a solution that encompasses those three elements.

Become an Entrepreneur

Be your own boss. Flexibility. Earn money without being physically present. Those are some of the reasons to pursue entrepreneurship. However, one of the main reasons is to pursue your passion while helping others in need. The potential for a substantial increase in income along with the potential tax deductions can give you the extra cash you need to accelerate your debt payoff goals.

However, entrepreneurship is not everyone's calling. And, that's okay. There are tons of side hustles you can begin almost immediately to increase your income! Here are 30+ side hustles you can start exploring today!

Side Hustles

1. Drive for Uber or Lyft

Driving for Uber or Lyft might be one of the most popular options people think of when they think of side hustles. Both of these companies are ride-sharing apps that have nearly replaced the need for taxis in most cities. Your main responsibility as a driver is to bring people to their respective destinations. This can entail picking someone up from their house to drop them off at the airport or picking them up after a late night out and dropping them back to their place of residence. To drive for Uber or Lyft you must be 21 years of age, have a valid driver's license, pass a screening process which includes a history of your driving record and a background check, and meet vehicle requirements for each company. What's great about this side hustle is that you set your own hours and can drive as little or as much as you would like. Simply turn on the app when you're available to pick a client up. Of course, the amount of money you earn is dependent on how much you drive, where you drive, and when you drive. And don't forget to factor in associated expenses such as gas and increased car maintenance costs. My cousin, Jerome, lives in a college town and earns between $450-$500/week before taxes driving Thursday-Saturday afternoons and nights. He worked for a total of 20-22 hours/week during the school year and earned almost $2,000/month of extra income!

2. Food Delivery Services (Uber Eats – Door Dash – Postmates)

If driving total strangers around in your car is not your cup of tea, there are other ways for you to use your vehicle to earn extra income. Uber Eats, DoorDash, and Postmates offer on-demand food delivery from local restaurants. Instead of picking up and dropping people off, you are picking up and delivering food. This is a great option for those who have older vehicles that do not meet the requirements for regular ride-sharing services. Like the ride-sharing apps, you can make yourself available as often as you would like. People pay for convenience and you could be earning some extra cash as you meet their needs.

3. Grocery Delivery Services (Instacart – Shipt)

Did you know people are even starting to order their groceries for delivery? This is becoming more popular particularly with the elderly community or full-time employees with extremely busy schedules. Instacart connects customers with shoppers to deliver fresh groceries to their door! You can become a full-service shopper where you shop for and deliver the groceries. This is an independent contractor position that will require you to have access to a vehicle. Or, you can become a part-time employee as an in-store shopper where you are only doing the shopping and a vehicle is not required. Both options offer you a flexible schedule and the opportunity to get paid to shop.

4. Pet Sit

If you have a pet, you know just how important they are to your family. When you have to head out of town for an extended period of time, you know just how stressful it can be to find a place to leave your pet and/or look for someone to come and feed and care for it. Well, if you love animals this is a great opportunity to help individuals who have those same needs. Pet sitting is the act of caring for someone's pet for a given time frame. This can either occur in the pet owner's home or in the home of the provider. You can pet sit for as little as a few hours a day for pet owners who work long hours and need someone to come and feed their animal. You can also pet sit over an extended period of time for pet owners who are out of town over the course of a few days or longer. You can market yourself on your local neighborhood website if you have one, social media, or work for a pet sitting business. The amount of money you can make varies. For example, when my cousins had to leave town for vacation, they had someone pet sit their beagle mix dog, Curry, for $20-$25/day for approximately 5 days. I also had a client who hired a pet sitter for 2 months at $15/day while she recovered from her arm injury. Her pet sitter earned $900 for those two months!

5. Walk Dogs

Wag walking and Rover are two dog walking businesses that connect pet owners to pet care professionals. If you love dogs, enjoy being active, and want to earn some extra income by taking them for a stroll outdoors, then this would be a great side hustle for you. Some of the requirements include being over 18 years of age, owning a smartphone, knowing basic dog commands, and being able to handle dogs of all sizes. For example, you can earn up to $20 for a 30-minute walk. Wag walking is currently accepting dog walking applicants in over 50 cities across the United States.

6. Give Music Lessons

Are you a musician? Know how to read and play music? There are many people who wish they were in your shoes and are looking to learn a few cords or strings on their favorite instrument. If you are able to teach and want to make some extra cash while doing something you love, then consider giving music lessons. You can schedule times in the evenings or on the weekends to work around your schedule.

7. Handyman/Mow Lawns

Are you handy around the house? Know how to do some basic repairs or just willing to get your hands dirty? You can pick up odds and end jobs in your neighborhood for some extra cash. Not a good handyman/woman, but know how to mow loans and trim hedges and shrubs? Start looking for some yards in your neighborhood that could use a little tender love and care and offer your services. Individuals in my community often ask for referrals on our neighborhood website for small household jobs they need to be completed. Make yourself available and you can be the trusted go-to person in your area. To expand your territory, you can sign up at www.taskrabbit.com to become a *tasker* and be notified of potential jobs in neighboring cities.

8. Babysit

Babysitting is one of the most common side hustles around. Babies are being born every day and the need for babysitters is an ongoing one. Faith picked up a babysitting job as a side hustle two to three days a week for a lovely young couple and their first-born baby. After working her full-time job, she heads to their home for a three-hour shift as the stay at home working mom runs errands and/or goes to the gym. The best part about it is that Faith loves children, so it doesn't even feel like work. Do you know anyone with children? Offer to babysit. I'm sure the parents would love to have a few hours of free time!

9. Waiter/Waitress or Bartender

Getting a job as a waiter/waitress or a bartender at a restaurant is the perfect opportunity for you to increase your income. Not only can you pick up a few hours at night during the week after working your full-time job, but you can also work on the weekends when restaurants are more packed and the tips are likely higher.

10. Tutor (Wyzant Online)

Math, English, and Science are three of the major subjects taught in school. If you are good at any of these subjects, you can become a tutor to high school students who need extra help understanding some of the concepts and who would benefit from 1-on-1 attention. Additionally, if you are currently in college, you could become a tutor to your peers in certain classes you're excelling in and earn money as part of work-study. I once tutored a 16-year-old who was struggling in English class for a few hours a week and earned $100/week. I also tutored a woman who was planning to return to school but was having difficulty with her prerequisite Anatomy & Physiology classes. The topics you tutor do not have to be limited to those traditional subjects.

Wyzant is an online-based service that matches tutors to students and allows you to choose the topic based on your qualifications and experience. You can work flexible hours and even set your own rates for what you think your expertise is worth.

11. Deliver Pizza

Pizza might be the most popular food item ordered out for delivery by people living in the U.S. Delivering pizza would be a great way to earn some extra cash for those willing to put in the work. If you can, choose nights and weekends where the earning potential from tips is higher. The best nights may be during concerts or major sporting events such as college and professional sports. If you live in a college town, a major city, near a big hotel, or an airport, you can be strategic and combine all of these factors to efficiently maximize your earning potential.

My friend, Brenden, works as a full-time banker during the day and has a side hustle as a pizza delivery guy by night. He was able to pay cash for a car by having the income from his pizza delivery job to supplement the income from his full-time job! Now, he and his family are using that extra income from the side hustle to pay off their debt at a much faster rate than they were able to before!

12. Clean Houses

If you don't mind getting your hands dirty, you can offer to clean houses or commercial buildings (offices, banks, etc.) for extra cash. Many people would love to have an ultra-clean home but do not have the time it takes to thoroughly clean it. Now, I'm not solely speaking of light dusting, cleaning the floors, and wiping the counters. I'm speaking of scrubbing the tub/shower, cleaning the toilets, cleaning the baseboards, and taking out the trash. Depending on the services performed you can earn anywhere between $150-$200 or more for a 3-bedroom, 2.5-bathroom home for the services described above. Be sure to have liability insurance in place for your protection and for a great selling point!

13. Car Flipping (Buy Low and Sell High)

If you're addicted to HGTV like I once was, you have probably seen many shows on flipping houses such as Flip or Flop, Flipping Virgins, or Rustic Rehab. Well, houses are not the only types of property you can flip. Flipping cars follows a similar business model of buying low, fixing the car and making it look nice (renovate), and selling high. If you love cars, know how to perform some of the work or know someone who can give you a deal on the labor, and/or have access to discounted parts then you can start using this side hustle to earn extra income. Most states will have a limit on the number of cars you can own in a given year. For the state of Georgia, the limit per person is six vehicles. That means if you're married, you can have a total of 12 vehicles in a given year between you and your spouse! Anything beyond that will require you to become a licensed dealer. If you're a novice, I would highly recommend you find a mentor who has experience doing this before venturing into this side hustle.

14. Refereeing or Coaching a Sport

If you love a certain sport and understand the rules of the game, consider becoming a referee or a coach! Sporting events are one of the most popular forms of entertainment known to man. Organized sports for children can start as early as age six and they all need referees and coaches. You can work for recreational leagues or at a local school in your community. Simply join an association in your community to receive the necessary information and training. The association will assign the games to you.

A basketball referee I know in Atlanta, GA gave me the following breakdown of earning potential from his side hustle. For recreation basketball, he typically referees 2-3 games per day/night.

Type of Referee	Amount Per Game
Recreation Basketball	$20-$25/game
High School Basketball Boys/Girls Varsity	$75/game
High School Basketball Boys/Girls Junior Varsity	$40/game
Middle School Basketball Boys/Girls	$30/game

Table 2.

My patient's daughter coaches in a soccer league and earns $50/hour. She typically conducts two hour-long practices per week and coaches two hour-long games on the weekends. Regardless of the sport, coaching and refereeing can earn you some extra cash in the evenings or on the weekends while simultaneously giving you front row access to a sport you enjoy!

15. Photography (Shutterstock, iStockPhoto, Fotolia, Big Stock Photo)

If you love to take pictures and have a decent camera, you can begin to use those skills as a side hustle. When people think of photography, they usually think of photography for weddings, fashion, and families/babies. However, did you know you can also become a street photographer, landscape photographer, travel photographer, food photographer, pet photographer, wildlife photographer, real estate and architecture photographer, underwater photographer, vehicle photographer, medical photographer, action and sport photographer, and so much more? Even more, you can sell your photos on microstock websites likes Shutterstock, iStockPhoto, Fotolia, and Big Stock Photo and earn extra cash! Once you're approved as a provider, these websites will not charge you to upload your photos but will take a percentage from each sale you make.

16. Personal Trainer

If you love to work out, have a solid foundation of the anatomy of the body, knowledge of general fitness with regard to exercise instruction and their progression, and have a good understanding of nutrition, then you can explore becoming a personal trainer as a side hustle. Most people would love to be physically fit but do not have the guidance they need. As a personal trainer, you can step in to meet that need and be creative by offering services that include meal planning and individualized plans to meet your client's specific goals. I know of someone who started hosting jump roping fitness classes and is using that as a side hustle to earn extra income.

17. Be a Plasma Donor

Did you know you can donate blood plasma to help someone in need and get paid for it? Plasma is the largest component of your blood content. People who have primary immune deficiencies and other blood disorders are in need of plasma as part of their medical treatment. Because plasma cannot be synthetically produced, these individuals rely on donors to donate the plasma. Some of the eligibility requirements include being over the age of 18, being in good health, and being at least 110 pounds. Once qualified, you can earn $200/month or more for frequent weekly donations depending on the company you choose. Keep in mind that donating plasma can take up to 2 hours of your time for each visit.

18. Focus Groups

Focus groups are one of the ways companies conduct market research studies. Through focus groups, you have the opportunity to test new products (food and phones, for example) before they make it to the market. Companies will use your opinions in order to improve upon their products. According to focusgroup.com, one can expect to earn between $75-$150 per focus group session. I included a list below of some available studies in Atlanta and Chicago with their respective pay rate as a reference at the time this book was written.

Chicago, IL — Available Studies

$ 100 One-on-One Interview - Chicago
Social Media - Ages 18-26

$ 200 In-home Interview - Chicago
Medical Conditions - Ages 25-44

$ 100 Focus Group - Chicago
Landscaping - Ages 25-65

$ 75 Focus Group - Chicago
Vaccines - Ages 19-45

$ 85 Focus Group - Chicago
Technology - Ages 19-55

Atlanta Buckhead, GA — Available Studies

$ 200 Focus Group - Atlanta Buckhead
Social Issues - Ages 23-69

$ 225 Focus Group - Atlanta Buckhead
Social Issues - 18-71

$ 75 Focus Grou - Atlanta Buckhead
Tobacco Products - Ages 24-45

$ 100 Focus Group - Atlanta Buckhead
Food Products - Ages 25-65

$ 225 Focus Group - Atlanta Buckhead
TV Viewing - Women ages 25-54

Figure 3. Retrieved from Home. (n.d.). Retrieved from https://www.focusgroup.com/ [6]

Side Hustles You Can Do From Home

19. FlexJobs

FlexJobs is a leading job search site specializing in remote, part-time, freelance, and flexible jobs. For a reasonably priced monthly or yearly subscription, FlexJobs gives you access to an up-to-date database of over 50 categories of job openings. They offer their members specialized job search checklists, one-on-one career coaching at a discounted rate, over 170 expert skills tests, thousands of articles, webinars with top hiring companies, educational guides, courses, and more! Visit flexjobs.com for more information.

20. Airbnb Rooms in Your Home or Apartment

Earning extra income doesn't always have to require you trading your time for money. You can earn additional income by renting out an extra room in your home or apartment (if your landlord allows). Airbnb has become a very popular alternative to hotel stays due to more reasonable prices. If you live in a desirable area, you may be able to capitalize by making your extra room available. Like hotels, prices will increase over the holidays, weekends, and when any major events are scheduled in your area. If you're comfortable, you can rent out the room while you're there or rent it out when you're out of town.

21. Rent Your Car on Turo

Did you know you could make extra money by renting out your car, truck, or van? Not only can you rent out a room in your apartment or home, but you can also rent out your car to earn extra cash! Turo is a peer-to-peer car rental service that allows private car owners to rent out their vehicles online or via a mobile interface. It's like an Airbnb, but for cars! As a host (the owner of the vehicle), it allows you to turn your depreciating car into an income stream! Other car sharing services include Getaround and Zipcar. Are you ready to earn some money by renting out your car?

22. Rent Out Your Parking Space or Parking Lot on AirGarage

If you work in the city or are heading there for a sports event or a fun day/night out, you know just how difficult it can be to find parking. Well, AirGarage provides homeowners and businesses with a platform to supplement their income by renting out their empty driveways and unused parking lots. With a fairly new inception date of only two years (2017), this company is planning to revolutionize the way people park at universities and in congested areas. If you have an extra parking space, this is an option that does not require any substantial ongoing effort. Now, this is what I call passive income!

23. Do Freelance Work (Fiverr, Guru, Upwork, 99designs, etc.)

If you are a freelancer or have skills such as writing, digital marketing, graphic design, or accounting that you can offer the global market then you are in for a treat. Many businesses and individuals are looking for ways to outsource some of their projects so they can be more efficient and reduce some of their burdens. Websites such as Fiverr, Guru, and Upwork make it easy to do that. These sites are freelancing platforms that connect individuals and businesses remotely for the purposes of accomplishing small or large tasks. We used one of these sites to create the logo for our business and also for our *Freedom On My Mind* t-shirts! While browsing, I saw listings across the spectrum ranging from voice-overs, editing, and designing a book cover to creating a website, video animation, administrative support, and legal support.

The company 99designs is another online marketplace specifically for graphic designing. Regardless of your skill level, you can begin to list your services with your corresponding prices today!

24. Take Surveys Online

Not everyone can afford to be away from home to earn extra income. I've had many people reach out and say they want to become debt free but are unable to work outside of the home either because they are single parents and cannot afford sitters or have a big family they need to tend to once they return home from their full-time jobs. If this is you, taking online surveys offers you the chance to earn additional income from the comfort of your home. Now, not all online surveys are created equal and there are many scams out there. Here are three I recommend checking out first: Survey Club, Survey Junkie, and Ipso-I Say. These companies generally look for certain demographics to complete specific surveys. They have options to pay you by check, gift cards, or via PayPal. Some other good options to try including Pureprofile, Swagbucks, InboxDollars, iPoll, Vindale Research, and Global Test Market.

25. Customer Interviews via Respondent

Not only can you get paid from taking surveys online, but you can also earn extra income by participating in research studies. Respondent.io offers companies the opportunity to recruit high-quality participants for market research studies. You can become one of those participants as long as you meet the occupational and demographic criteria set forth by the companies. According to Respondent.io, the average customer interview length is 30 minutes and the average pay is $140/hour!

26. Become a Social Media Manager

Social Media Manager? Does this really exist? Those are the exact same questions I asked when I first heard of this position. To my surprise, this is actually a real job! And you can do it full time if you wanted to, earning a salary between $34,000-$56,000 according to Payscale.com. But hold your horses if you think the number of likes you have on Instagram and Facebook give you the credibility to manage someone else's or another business' account. So, what exactly do social media managers do? They do a whole lot! Their primary responsibility is to curate a brand's social channels by creating, managing, maintaining, and validating content relevant to the brand's areas of expertise. Aside from creating social media content, they create/implement social media strategy and execute digital marketing campaigns. They then analyze the results from those campaigns by measuring and proving return on investment (ROI), monitor and respond to audience comments, collaborate and partner with other brands, and so much more!

Some of the skills needed to be a social media manager include, but are not limited to, top-notch writing skills, customer service skills, social media expertise and understanding how content works on social media, strategy planning, branding/marketing experience, and research. You can build a portfolio via your own social media accounts to market yourself if you think you have what it takes to make some additional income this way. If you're on the fence and need an extra push, you can look for an online course to help you hone in on your skills with a simple google search.

27. Affiliate Marketing via a Blog or YouTube Channel

Merely starting a blog will not earn you money, but having

a blog people are really interested in is one of the most common platforms you can use to conduct affiliate marketing. What exactly is affiliate marketing? It is the process of partnering with a business or an individual to promote their products and/or services. In exchange for referring your readers or visitors to the company via a click ad link, you have the opportunity to earn a commission each time the customer purchases a product and/or service.

Here are some helpful tips I would suggest if you're just starting out:

- Be genuine about helping your customers rather than selling.
- Start with two to three products.
- Test out the products/service you are referring your customers to.
- Track your sales to see where they came from in order to improve upon your outcomes.

You can also earn money on your blog via the products you sell, services you offer, ad income, and sponsored advertisements. During my research, I've come across two individuals who earn $100,000/month through their respective blogs! Crazy, right?

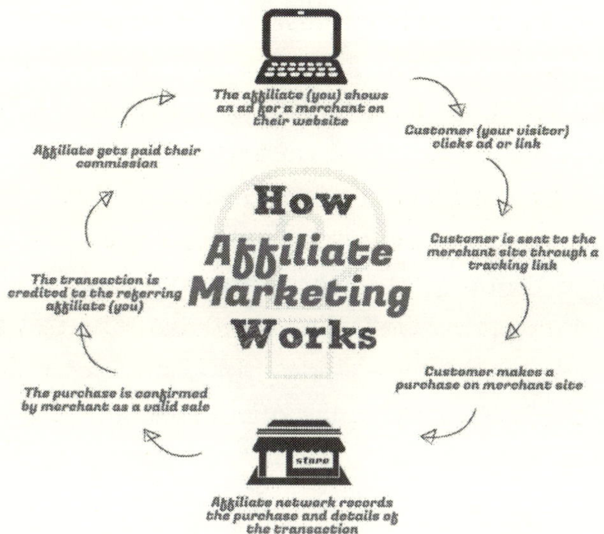

Figure 4. Retrieved from https://successfulbusinessonline.org/affiliate-marketing [7]

28. Selling on Amazon, Ebay, Facebook Marketplace, Poshmark, or Craigslist

This side hustle is self-explanatory and does not require much skill beyond the ability to take a picture, use the internet or a mobile app to upload it, and write a brief description of the item you plan to sell. If you haven't taken inventory of your belongings in a while, this would be a great time to search your closet or rummage through your basement for items you have not used or worn that may still have some value. As always, be cautious of meeting with people from these websites if scheduling an in-person pick-up or drop-off.

29. Virtual Assistant (VA)

Virtual assistants are becoming a vital asset in the day-today operations of businesses nowadays. Rather than hiring part-time secretaries or administrative assistants, busy entrepreneurs and busy managers are choosing to outsource specific administrative or technical tasks to virtual assistants on an as-needed basis. A virtual assistant is an individual who works remotely (usually from home) for multiple clients performing various tasks. Their skills vary, but their primary job is to provide support to those professionals for tasks including, but certainly not limited to, fielding phone calls, email management, scheduling, data entry, accounting and bookkeeping, conducting research, generating reports, you name it! Some virtual assistants specialize in certain fields like marketing and public relations or event and travel planning.

My cousin, Mike, is a certified public accountant (CPA) who recently started his own accounting company to serve small businesses in his local community in Boston, MA. He hires VA's as needed to perform routine tasks for his company such as drafting instructional documentation for future new hires, basic calendar management, and filling out-of-state power of attorney forms for him to review.

You can market yourself as a VA on sites like Upwork or Fiverr, which were mentioned earlier. While doing research on this particular side hustle, I came across a woman who earns $10,000/month (yes, you read that correctly) as a full-time VA! So, if you have good organizational skills, this might be the perfect opportunity for you to earn extra income from the comfort of your home.

30. Teach Kids English Online with VIPKID

VIPKID is an online education company matching Chinese students with teachers in North America. It was voted #1 by FlexJobs in Forbes magazine's *2018 list of the Top 100 Companies For Remote Jobs.*[8] With this job, you have the flexibility to create your own schedule and work as many hours as you would like. VIPKID provides you with all of the lesson plans and all you need is access to a computer and the passion/skills to teach children. According to the VIPKID website, you can earn $14-$22/hour from the comfort of your home. A person who works for this company told me she brings home $1,000-$1,500/month by working 15 hours per week. Another person said she earned $892 her first month of working and $1,500 during the second month. This is a promising side hustle for those who have the skill to teach. Visit their website at www.vipkidteachers.com for more information.

Bonus Side Hustle List

1. Network Marketing – Multilevel marketing business model that depends on a network of distributors. Think Avon, Mary Kay, and AdvoCare.

2. Lifeguard – Work at a local pool or gym. You can even become a lifeguard at a waterpark or beach!

3. Amazon Flex – Earn between $18-$25/hour delivering packages for Amazon. Imagine how much you could earn during the holiday seasons!

4. Event Staffing Jobs for sporting events, concerts,

festivals, theater shows, etc.

5. Create Facebook Ads and Google Ads.

6. Dosh App – Earn money on purchases by linking your card and referring people to sign up!

7. Custodial Staff – Offer after-hour cleaning services at doctor's offices, banks, therapy offices, etc.

8. Arise – A virtual call center you can do from home. Visit www.arise.com for more info.

9. Become a Loan Signing Agent and Notary.

10. Catering – Become a catering staff in an on-demand industry. Catering companies are always hiring!

11. User Testing – Get paid to test websites and offer feedback. Visit www.usertesting.com for more info.

12. Mystery Shopping – Buy in secret and document your experience via Secret Shopper (www.secretshopper.com) and Field Agent (www.fieldagent.net).

13. Sell crafts and artwork on Etsy.

14. Create an online course – Become an expert in your niche and create courses that offer tremendous value!

15. Resume Writing – Are you good at writing resumes? You can offer your services on professional websites like LinkedIn!

Additional Work From Home Options

In no particular order, here are some additional resources

you can explore to find remote jobs you can do from the comfort of your home.

1. Remoteok.io
2. Ratracerebellion.com
3. Workingnomads.co/jobs
4. Remote.co
5. Weworkremotely.com
6. Virtualvocations.com
7. Remotive.io
8. Angel.co

This list is by no means an exhaustive one and not every side hustle listed here will work for everyone. This is simply a starting point for you to discover different ways you can potentially earn extra income to pay off your debt at a much faster rate. I know all of the options mentioned on this list may not appeal to you, but I am sure there are a few you can at least give a try. If not, I can guarantee you that there are many more options out there. I made sure to include options for the busy parent or stay at home mom, as well as the single person who may have more time to spare. Remember, this is not the time to make excuses or the time to seek convenience. Hustle implies being assertive and it will require you to make some sacrifices in order to make it work. I am a firm believer that anyone can earn extra income if they put enough effort into it.

INSIDE SCOOP 

*I earned **$27,339.44** (before taxes) from my side hustle in 2018. Faith earned **$39,387.52** (before taxes) from her side hustle alone in 2018! No, this is not a typo. We earned that amount by working our butts off with our side hustles!*

Now that you are aware of these options, you can start to put in the work yourself. What is your excuse? Remember, the purpose of side hustles is not intended for it to become your career. It is a means to an end. The end goal is being debt free, living life on your own terms, and leaving a legacy behind for the generations who come after you. Decreasing our expenses and increasing our income were two major ways we were able to make a huge dent in our debt payoff goals! I hope this chapter has equipped you with the strategies you need to implement in order to make a huge dent in yours!

ACTIVITY: MAXIMIZE YOUR CASH FLOW

Reflect on your budget and lifestyle. List 3 areas where you can decrease your expenses.

1. _______________________________

2. _______________________________

3. _______________________________

List three side hustles you can realistically do and apply for this week to boost your income!

1. _______________________________
2. _______________________________
3. _______________________________

Critical Thinking Questions

1. What's the hardest part about decreasing your expenses?
2. How much faster would you be able to reach your goals if you increase your income?

The BULLETPROOF Steps in Review

STEP 1: DREAM

Establish your reason(s) for wanting to be debt free. This is the *why* behind the *what*. Your DREAM is the reason you start your journey, the reason you do not quit, the reason your spouse gets on board, and so much more! This is the first step toward debt freedom.

STEP 2: KNOW HOW MUCH YOU OWE

Identify your target number. This is your debt-free goal amount. List all of the lending institutions you owe, along with the current balance and interest rates for each loan. You cannot effectively strategize unless you know the exact amount you're up against.

STEP 3: BUDGET

Create a plan for your money. Give each dollar you earn an *assignment* before you ever receive your paycheck. This way, all of your money is accounted for and not one penny is falling through the cracks. The formula is simple: Earn an income, prioritize by telling your money where it goes, and stick to your plan.

STEP 4: STARTER EMERGENCY FUND

Establish a starter emergency fund as a layer of protection and buffer against life's unexpected events as you diligently execute a plan to pay off your debt. This will ensure you remain on track on your journey and do not get further into debt. Emergencies will happen, but you do not have to be unprepared.

STEP 5: DECREASE EXPENSES + INCREASE INCOME

Spend less than you earn. Cut back on everything that is eating away at your budget. Create new income streams to generate more cash. Decreasing your expenses and increasing your income are two surefire ways to maximize cash flow and accelerate your debt payoff goals.

Chapter 8

STEP 6: ATTACK YOUR DEBT
Show No Mercy

John Kreese: Fear does not exist in this dojo, does it?

Cobra Kai: No, Sensei!

John Kreese: Pain does not exist in this dojo, does it?

Cobra Kai: No, Sensei!

John Kreese: Defeat does not exist in this dojo, does it?

Cobra Kai: No, Sensei!

John Kreese: Prepare! What do we study here?

Cobra Kai: The way of the fist, sir!

John Kreese: And what is that way?

Cobra Kai: Strike first, strike hard, no mercy, sir!

John Kreese: I can't hear you!

Cobra Kai: Strike first, strike hard, no mercy, sir!

- Cobra Kai (Karate Kid TV Series)

YOUR JOURNEY TO DEBT FREEDOM began by *dreaming* of all the possibilities and opportunities a debt-free future could offer you. Your *why* became the breeding ground for the change you desired to see in your life and in your finances. Establishing your *why* by dreaming compelled you to act. So, you took the next step by *discovering how much you owe and writing down your debt-free goal amount.* BULLETPROOF STEPS 3-5 required you to take control of your finances by mastering the art of *budgeting*, establishing your *starter emergency fund*, and using the double-edged sword of *decreasing expenses and increasing your income.* You are now ready to enter the last phase of the program: ATTACK YOUR DEBT. It is time to take all of the money you were able to free up in BULLETPROOF STEPS 3 and 5 and put it ALL toward your debt! Wait. You didn't think that extra income was for you to splurge on a nice vacation, did you? No, all of the sacrifices I am imploring you to make are for you to get out of debt and to get out as fast as you can! It is during this step that you can begin to chip away at your debt, steadily and faithfully.

However, paying off debt is not as simple as it sounds. It is a process that will require a plan, mental toughness, discipline, commitment, strategy, and intensity you may have never experienced before. Your ability to navigate the various challenges of this step will determine how effective you will ultimately be and how much progress you will make toward your goals. The primary objective of this chapter is to teach you how to execute ATTACK mode.

Though this book is about paying off debt in general, the emphasis is given particularly to non-mortgage debt. You should focus on paying your mortgage off early only after you have taken care of all other debt and after some important financial milestones are in place. I will discuss this a bit later in the chapter. When paying off your debt, you should prioritize paying the IRS any back taxes you owe them first. Not doing so will cost you with regard to late penalties, the accrual of interest on your debt, and even the seizing of your assets! Take a look at this excerpt from the IRS website.

> The IRS may levy (seize) assets such as wages, bank accounts, social security benefits, and retirement income. The IRS also may seize your property (including your car, boat, or real estate) and sell the property to satisfy the tax debt. In addition, any future federal tax refunds or state income tax refunds that you're due may be seized and applied to your federal tax liability.[1]

Do you see why you need to pay your IRS debt immediately? Aside from satisfying your debt to the IRS, there is no order of preference given to all other non-mortgage debts such as student loans, medical bills, car loans, personal loans, etc. How you prioritize which debt to pay off first depends on which payoff method you decide to use. We will discuss two of the most widely known methods: The **Debt Avalanche** and the **Debt Snowball**.

Debt Avalanche

An avalanche is described as a mass of snow, ice, soil or rocks (or a mixture of these components) that falls suddenly and rapidly down the inclined slope of a mountainside. According to the National Geographic, avalanches can reach speeds up to 80mph within 5 seconds, as volumes of rubble rush violently down the steep slope, destroying everything along its path.[2] Well, the debt avalanche is a type of accelerated debt payoff plan that works in a similar fashion. In this method, you are asked to pay off your debt in the order of *the highest interest rate to the lowest interest rate*, irrespective of the dollar amount. Before you start to pay down your debt aggressively, it is important that you are current, or become current, on all of your monthly bills and loans. Below is a step-by-step breakdown of how you would execute this payoff method.

- List your debt in the order of *the highest interest rate to the lowest interest rate*, irrespective of the dollar amount.
- Pay the minimum payments on all debts. It is important for you to pay the minimum payments on every debt to avoid incurring late fees or defaulting on your loans.
- Allocate any extra cash you were able to

free up by decreasing the expenses in your budget and/or any additional income you receive from your side hustles toward the debt with the *highest interest rate first.*
- Once you pay off that particular loan, take the minimum payment you were paying on it, as well as any additional cash, and apply it toward the next loan on your list.
- Continue to work your way down from the highest interest rate to the lowest interest rate until all debts are paid off.

For example, let's say you have the following debts:

- Sallie Mae student loan balance of $38,000 with an interest rate of 10.50%
- Store Credit Card balance of $1,625 with an interest rate of 12.99%
- Auto Loan balance of $5,000 with an interest rate of 5.00%
- Visa Credit Card balance of $5,500 with an interest rate of 21.99%

Your debt should be listed in the order of *the highest interest rate to the lowest interest rate.* In this case, the Visa Credit Card will become your top priority! See the following table.

Name	Balance	Min. Payment	Interest Rate	Type
Loan 1: Visa Credit Card	$5,500	$105	21.99%	Credit Card
Loan 2: Store Credit Card	$1,625	$25	12.99%	Credit Card
Loan 3: Sallie Mae Student Loans	$38,000	$346	10.50%	Student Loan
Loan 4: Auto Loan	$5,000	$374	5.00%	Auto Loan

Table 1.

Total minimum payment: $850/month

As mentioned earlier, this method requires you to pay the minimum payments on all of your debts. Once minimum payments are made on all of your debts, you would focus your energy on the debt with the *highest interest rate first* – the Visa Credit Card. This is where you can begin adding any extra cash you have above your minimum payment toward your debt in order to aggressively pay it off.

For example, let's say you are able to earn $150 in additional income from side hustles. You would pay the

$105 minimum payment on the Visa Credit Card plus the additional $150 until that debt is paid off.

Name	Balance	Min. Payment	Interest Rate	Type
Loan 1: Visa Credit Card	$5,500	$105 + ($150 extra)	**21.99%**	Credit Card
Loan 2: Store Credit Card	$1,625	$25	**12.99%**	Credit Card
Loan 3: Sallie Mae Student Loans	$38,000	$346	**10.50%**	Student Loan
Loan 4: Auto Loan	$5,000	$374	**5.00%**	Auto Loan

Table 2.

Total minimum payment: $850/month
Extra Payment: $150

Once the Visa Credit card is paid off, you would take the minimum payment you were paying on it ($105) plus the $150 extra cash, and apply it to the next debt on your list with the second highest interest rate – the Store Credit Card. You would now have a total of $280 to apply to the Store Credit Card, including its $25 minimum payment.

Name	Balance	Min. Payment	Interest Rate	Type
~~Loan 1: Visa Credit Card~~	~~$5,500~~	~~$105 + ($150 extra)~~	**21.99%**	~~Credit Card~~
Loan 2: Store Credit Card	$1,625	$ 25 $105 +$150 =**$280**	12.99%	Credit Card
Loan 3: Sallie Mae Student Loans	$38,000	$346	**10.50%**	Student Loan
Loan 4: Auto Loan	$5,000	$374	**5.00%**	Auto Loan

Table 3.

Total minimum payment: $850/month
Extra Payment: $255

Each time you pay off a debt, you would roll the payments down successively to the next loan. Just like an avalanche!

Mathematically speaking, the debt avalanche is the fastest way to pay off debt in the long run. With this option, your total amount of debt would be paid off in a shorter time frame and you would pay less money in interest over the life of the loan. Proponents of this method say it is the more efficient way to pay off debt and thus should be deemed the correct and only way everyone should pay off their debt. However, most people know money involves more than just pure math. There is a psychological component to it as well. In fact, personal finance is 80% behavior and only 20% math. People have personal relationships with money and are often emotionally invested in it. For this reason, they do not always make the most rational decisions when it comes to money. Although the total amount of debt you owe would be paid off faster with the debt avalanche in the long run, it may take longer to pay off the first initial loan with the highest interest rate. As a result, remaining motivated becomes a legitimate concern on the journey to debt freedom using this method. Hence, the reason others choose to do the debt snowball.

Debt Snowball

The debt snowball is notoriously known as Dave Ramsey's preferred/recommended way to pay off debt. Like the debt avalanche, the reference to snow is used as an analogy to describe how this method works. When I lived in Boston, MA for a few years as a kid, the winter season was one of my favorite seasons of the year. Not only because of Christmas, but because of the many hours my cousins and I would get to spend outside playing in the snow! If you grew up in a place where it snowed, you remember those exact feelings of excitement and anticipation as you were putting on layers of clothing, your winter jacket, snow boots, gloves, scarf, and you can't forget the beanie! From making a snowman to making snow angels, sledding on trash can lids down the hill (talk about being creative on a budget), tasting the snow, and snow fights, playing in the snow was a child's dream! One of my cousin's greatest feats one winter was making a giant snowball. And, it didn't magically appear like it's portrayed in the movies. He had to be patient with the process and he had to be comfortable starting small. Below are his exact words describing what he remembered about his childhood experience:

> *Once you have a solid little snowball that is hard and compact, you can trust that the additional snow you add on will stick. Slowly, but surely, the snowball gets bigger because of your patience and because you know that the original small snowball won't fall apart. Before you know it, you've got yourself a massive snowball! - Mike Moise*

Unlike the debt avalanche, the debt snowball requires you to list and pay your debt in the order of *the smallest debt amount to the largest debt amount*, irrespective of the interest rate. This method addresses the psychological and emotional aspect of money by focusing on the boost of confidence that can be attained by attacking the debt with the smallest amount first. The idea is that by paying off your small debts fast, you would be motivated to continue because you would see the quick progress being made on your debt payoff goals. Each time you pay off a debt, you would move to the next one, using the money you spent paying the previous debt to add on top of the following debt's payment. Eliminating the payments from the smaller debts will progress into larger amounts of cash being available to throw at the higher debt amounts on your list. That small initial payment amount gradually becomes this giant amount – just like a snowball! And, the momentum you would gain from those small victories would propel you to an accelerated debt payoff plan you can actually stick to! Remember, you must be current on all of your monthly bills and loans before you start to pay extra toward your debt. Here is a step-by-step breakdown of how the debt snowball works.

- List your debt in the order of *the smallest debt amount to the largest debt amount,* irrespective of interest rate or loan service provider.

- Pay the minimum payments on all debts. It's important for you to pay the minimum payments on every debt to avoid incurring late fees or defaulting on your loans.

- Allocate any extra cash you free up by decreasing the expenses in your budget and/or any additional income you receive from your side hustles toward the debt with the *smallest amount first.*

- Once you pay off that particular loan, take the minimum payment you were paying on it, as well as any additional cash, and apply it toward the following loan on your list.

- Continue to work your way from the smallest amount to the largest amount until all debts are paid off.

Let's use the same loans in the example for the debt avalanche. Only this time, they will be listed in the order of *the smallest debt amount to the largest debt amount* rather than focusing on the interest rates.

Name	Balance	Min. Payment	Interest Rate	Type
Loan 2: Store Credit Card	$1,625	$25	12.99%	Credit Card
Loan 4: Auto Loan	$5,000	$374	5.00%	Auto Loan
Loan 1: Visa Credit Card	$5,500	$105	21.99%	Credit Card
Loan 3: Sallie Mae Student Loans	$38,000	$346	10.50%	Student Loan

Table 4.

Total minimum payment: $850/month

When you're working the debt snowball, you are required to make minimum payments on all of your debts. Once all minimum payments are made, you will focus all of your energy on the debt with the *smallest amount first* – the Store Credit Card. Any additional cash you are able to free up or earn will go toward this debt. Here is the breakdown if you are able to earn $150 in additional income from side hustles to add to your payment.

Loan 2 Store Credit Card Minimum Payment – $25 You would add $150 and pay a total of $175 per month until this debt is paid off.

Name	Balance	Min. Payment	Interest Rate	Type
Loan 2: Store Credit Card	**$1,625**	$25 + ($150 extra)	12.99%	Credit Card
Loan 4: Auto Loan	**$5,000**	$374	5.00%	Auto Loan
Loan 1: Visa Credit Card	**$5,500**	$105	21.99%	Credit Card
Loan 3: Sallie Mae Student Loans	**$38,000**	$346	10.50%	Student Loan

Table 5.

Once the Store Credit Card is paid off, you would then roll $175 to the next debt. You would take the minimum payment you were paying on it ($25) plus the $150 extra cash and roll it over to the next debt on your list – the Auto Loan. You would end up paying $549 each month on the Auto Loan ($25 minimum payment from Store Credit Card + $150 extra income from side hustles + $374 minimum payment on the Auto Loan). You would repeat this process until you pay off all of your debts. See the table below.

Name	Balance	Min. Payment	Interest Rate	Type
~~Loan 2: Store Credit Card~~	~~$1,625~~	~~$25~~ ~~+ $150~~ ~~(extra)~~	~~12.99%~~	~~Credit Card~~
Loan 4: Auto Loan	$5,000	$374 $25 +$150 =$594	5.00%	Auto Loan
Loan 1: Visa Credit Card	$5,500	$105	21.99%	Credit Card
Loan 3: Sallie Mae Student Loans	$38,000	$346	10.50%	Student Loan

Table 6.

In the examples above, both the debt avalanche and debt snowball have the same minimum monthly payments of $850 due on the accounts. Both examples also use the extra $150 from side hustles to throw at the debt. By using the debt avalanche you would save *$326.29* over the life of the loan, however, it would take you **six months** longer to pay off your first debt. See the chart below.

Payoff Comparison		
The avalanche method saves you **$326.29** of interest in the long run. The snowball method pays off your first debt **6 months** sooner.		
Strategy Payoff date	Payoff Interest paid	First debt payoff Total paid
Snowball 07/06/2024	68 months $17,423	10 months $67,548
Avalanche 07/06/2024	68 months $17,096	16 months $67,221

Table 7.

To find a calculator that compares the debt snowball and debt avalanche methods, simply google search "Dough Roller Debt Snowball and Avalanche Payoff Calculator."[3]

Debt Avalanche or Debt Snowball?

Figure 1.

So, which is the better method? Wouldn't you love if I just gave you the answer? Well, that would be too easy! When Faith and I began our journey to debt freedom in the summer of 2017, we started paying off our debt using the debt avalanche method. I tend to be analytical, so I strongly suggested this method because the math made it clear this was the more efficient way. Our debt would be paid off faster and we would pay less in interest over the life of our loans. Say no more! So, we embarked on the journey attacking the loans with the highest interest rates first. It took us a while to pay off those first few student loans and we soon found ourselves struggling to remain the course. Faith, in particular, expressed her frustrations early on. Though she bought into the plan to pay off our debt as aggressively as we could, she was initially hesitant. She had only been employed in her first career job out of school for three months before we got married and started our debt-free journey. So, she wanted to see the results behind of all the sacrifices we were making and all of the long hours we were working. Telling her how much extra money we were able to put toward the loans each month wasn't enough. She wanted to see the debt eliminated at a faster rate. When I chose the debt avalanche, I failed to realize the importance behind the psychology of debt and the psychology of human behavior. And, can you believe I majored in psychology as an undergrad?

After several discussions, we decided to switch to the debt snowball in January of 2018. We wanted to see if this method would give us the added boost we needed on our journey. And, it absolutely did! We paid off two loans in the first month. In February, we paid off two more. We were eliminating our loans at a much faster pace than before. It felt so good to cross the loans off of our list. I noticed a shift in our relationship; Faith was less annoyed and more motivated. Her confidence in the process grew. Those small victories gave us a sense of accomplishment and developed an urge to do more so we could continue to see the impact. We signed up for more shifts at our side hustles and in four short months, we were able to pay off eight loans totaling over $32,000! Switching to the debt snowball was a total game changer for us! It was this debt payoff method that accelerated our debt payoff total to $104,221.89 in just 12 months!

Which plan you decide to use is ultimately a matter of personal preference. However, I highly recommend the debt snowball on your journey to debt freedom. Regardless of how financially literate you are, you cannot dismiss the psychological and emotional component to debt and money. Think about the reasons most people get into debt in the first place. People tend to do what *feels good* vs. what *works best*. They want something they don't have the money for, lack discipline, can't seem to delay gratification, fail to plan ahead, and so they borrow. Because getting into debt is more often a result of human behavior and emotion rather than rational thinking, I propose that the emotional being of the person needs to be targeted when seeking to get out of debt. This is more so accomplished during the debt snowball method.

Research conducted on this topic further supports this claim. A study by Kettle et al. (2016) found that individuals with multiple credit card debt with large balances became more motivated to pay off their debt when they started with the smaller debts first.[4] Furthermore, a study published in the *Journal of Marketing Research* titled "Can Small

Victories Help Win the War? Evidence from Consumer Debt Management" found that individuals are more likely to stick to their plan to eliminate their debt if they focus on the smaller balances first.[5]

Even when people do begin to rationalize and realize the predicament they've put themselves in, the total amount of debt they owe overwhelms them and often paralyzes them from taking action. That's a big reason we don't recommend you start your journey with the numbers but rather by dreaming! It's easy to become discouraged when it takes a long time to pay down debt; you will either lose steam or stop paying altogether. It may take even longer to pay off your first debt if your higher interest loans also have the highest balances. However, the debt snowball method focuses on easy to conquer debts first that will target that inner part of you that desires something to feel good and be proud about. Your quick victories on those smaller and more manageable debts will give you all of the motivation you need to progressively knock out your debt and remain steadfast on this debt-free emotional roller coaster.

In the next few sections, I will briefly introduce and explain some options available to individuals in debt. These options offer selling points of lowering your monthly payments or lowering your debt altogether. But do they really work? Let's see how promising they are.

The Truth About Debt Consolidation

As stated in Chapter 4, it is not uncommon for individuals in debt to have multiple loans with multiple service providers. Dealing with all of these accounts, which often have different due dates and different loan repayment terms, can become stressful and difficult to keep up with. Debt consolidation offers you the opportunity to combine all of your debts, including student loans, auto loans, credit cards, and medical bills via a debt consolidation loan or a personal loan. The end result is one single monthly payment instead of multiple payments. The interest rate is usually fixed and is determined by the weighted average of the interest rates of the loans being consolidated. Debt consolidation companies will promise one single, lower monthly payment as one of the primary ways to entice borrowers to sign up. However, part of the reason for the lower monthly payment is due to a longer repayment term that may cost you more in the long run. Now, while a lower monthly payment may sound appealing initially, you will quickly realize the cons outweigh the pros if you dig a little deeper.

Pros

- Makes it easier to manage your debts.
- Offers a lower monthly payment.
- You can consolidate multiple federal education loans into one loan at no cost to you with the Department of Education.

Cons

- Debt consolidation does not change or reduce the amount of debt you owe. You are responsible for paying your debt in full.

- Debt consolidation usually increases the length of time you have to repay your loans, resulting in you having to make more payments and also paying more interest over the life of the loan.

- Consolidating your loans may cause you to lose out on some borrower benefits and perks you previously had on your loans such as interest rate discounts.

- Any outstanding interest you have on your loans at the time you decide to consolidate will be added to your new original balance. Interest would then accrue on a higher principal balance than before.

- There are fees associated with consolidating your loans through a third-party lender. These fees can be rolled into your new loan amount, resulting in a higher balance than you previously had.

- It robs you of the opportunity to work the debt snowball as you would now have one big lump sum loan instead of multiple loans.

- By having one single loan, you would no longer have the opportunity to reduce your monthly payments. On the contrary, if you had multiple loans, you could reduce your monthly payment each time you pay off a loan.

Though consolidating your loans may seem to make life easier, that reason alone does not suffice to pursue it as an option. There are other ways for you to get organized and make your debts more manageable. We mentioned how important it is to factor in the psyche of individuals who are paying off debt earlier in the chapter. Individuals are more likely to stay the course of paying off their debt if they are targeting smaller loan balances first. You would miss out on that opportunity if you consolidated your loans. Imagine what would happen if a person had *one consolidated loan* amount of $50,000-$100,000 compared to *ten smaller loans* totaling that same amount. It's not hard to understand how that person could become easily discouraged on their journey because of that one large debt amount. Debt consolidation would rob them of the opportunity to work the snowball method and gain those small victories. Because of this and what's listed in the *cons* section above, I discourage this option. Consolidating your loans does nothing to address the behavior that got you into debt in the first place and it does not push you any closer to debt freedom.

Would you rather pay off **ONE loan** with a balance of $50,000?

OR

Would you rather pay off **TEN loans** with a balance of $5,000 each?

The Truth About Refinancing

In Chapter 3, we discussed the impact interest rates have on your loans. Interest on loans accrue daily in most cases and if you take your time paying back your debt, it can become very costly, very quickly. Another popular avenue offered by companies to lower your monthly payments is the option to refinance your loans. When you refinance, your new lender pays off your existing loans and replaces them with a new loan at a lower interest rate. Refinancing allows you to adjust the terms of your loans, the primary incentive being a reduced interest rate. Contrary to popular belief, the interest rate you received when you first took out the loan may not be etched in stone forever for some loans. If the government reduces interest rates or if your credit score improves, you may have the option to seek a lower fixed interest rate by refinancing your loans. This is particularly advantageous for individuals with high-interest rates and/or variable interest rates. For example, reducing your interest rate from a 10% variable rate to a 6% fixed rate would result in significant savings! You can choose to refinance an individual loan or multiple loans. There are four types that are typically eligible for refinancing: student loans, auto loans, credit card balances, and mortgage loans.[6]

Student Loans

Federal and private student loans can both qualify for refinancing. The Department of Education does not offer student loan refinancing; however, you can find many third-party lenders that do. It is important to note that refinancing federal loans will cause them to be disqualified from government benefits such as income-driven repayment plans.

Credit Cards

Credit card refinancing is the process of moving one credit card debt to another credit card with more favorable interest rates. You will likely see this offered in the form of a balance transfer with a 0% introductory rate for the first 12-18 months. This is the primary way banks lure consumers to sign up. However, the offer of a 0% introductory rate is only beneficial if you take advantage and pay off your debt within that introductory window. After that period, your interest rate will usually return to a double-digit number that may be higher than your current rate.

Auto Loans

Auto loans are more difficult to refinance due to the fact that most people are upside down on their vehicles, meaning they owe more on their vehicle than it is worth. It will be difficult to find a company willing to refinance this type of loan, especially if the value of the car is less than the amount you are looking to refinance. Also, lenders typically stay away from older, high-mileage vehicles. If your car situation is more favorable than what is being described here, you can shop around for potential deals.

Mortgage Loan

As with the other types of loans, the goal of refinancing your mortgage loan is to obtain a lower interest rate. This type of refinancing has the opportunity to save you thousands of dollars simply due to the fact that mortgage balances are typically much higher and the loan repayment term longer. It is important to note that refinancing will start your timeframe all over again. For example, let's say you are in year 3 out of 15 of paying off your house at the time you choose to refinance. If you take out another 15-year loan, you would have made payments for 18 years in total instead of 15.

I am not entirely against refinancing your loans as long as you do not consolidate your loans at the same time. Again, you do not want to give up the option to work the debt snowball on your loans. The decision to refinance depends on several factors. The biggest factor to consider is how much money you could potentially *save* on your loans. For example, my colleague Kyle was able to reduce the interest rate on his $80,000 student loans from 7% to 3%! That's a ton of savings! Other factors to consider are:

- Third-party lenders charge loan origination fees and balance transfer fees to refinance your loans. These fees can range from 1 to 6 percent of the new loan amount.

- Refinancing into a lower monthly payment may extend your loan repayment term, resulting in you paying more over the life of the loan.

If you're able to reduce the interest rate on your loan(s), refinancing could potentially result in significant savings for you. Take your time to understand the rates being offered. A low fixed rate is better than a low variable rate as your monthly payments would not change. Lastly, choose a shorter repayment term to avoid paying more in interest.

The Truth About Debt Settlement

There are many reasons one might default on their loans. Some reasons are external and out of that person's control and some are self-inflicting. Those reasons can include financial hardships from medical conditions, divorce, or accidents/injuries resulting in disability. On the other hand, some individuals have incomes that are too low to keep up with their payments and others are just outright negligent. Regardless of your personal circumstance, having debts in collections is never a good thing. I'm sure you're tired of dodging their calls and receiving debt collection letters in the mail. Well, this is when debt settlement companies come to save the day. Have you heard of those radio ads of debt settlement companies claiming they can eliminate a consumer's debt by settling with the lender for a mere fraction of the debt owed?

Debt settlement is a negotiated agreement in which a lender legally agrees to settle and accept less than the full amount owed on the account. Why would a lender ever agree to those terms? Well, this usually occurs when the lender believes it is unrealistic a borrower will ever be able to pay back his/her debt. Rather than not receiving anything at all, the lender may sometimes agree on a lower amount. Sounds like a good deal, right? Not quite. On the surface, debt settlement is presented as an alternative to bankruptcy that rescues you from all of your debt nightmares. However, there are many dangers involved in pursuing this option. Here are some you should be aware of:

- **You will ruin your credit:** In order for lenders to agree to accept less than the full amount owed, your account must be past due for at least a few months. If it isn't already past due, debt settlement companies will advise you to stop making payments on your loans. Instead, they will tell you to open a settlement account with them and allocate your funds into that account until it builds up enough cash to make a decent offer to your lender. In the meantime, lenders will report your delinquent accounts to the credit bureaus, which would result in a bad credit score. Furthermore, if you settle your account (and that's a big if), it will remain on your credit history for seven years! Future lenders will be able to look at your credit history and see that you left the last company hanging. Not good!

- **You will be taxed on the amount forgiven:** Any debt forgiven above $600 becomes a taxable event. For example, if someone settles a $15,000 debt for $7,000, the forgiven amount of $8,000 becomes taxable.

- **Debt settlement companies charge you fees:** Debt settlement companies will either charge you a percentage of the settled debt or a percentage of the forgiven amount. Let's say you settled the account you owed $15,000 on for $7,000. Some debt settlement companies may charge you a 25% fee on the settled amount ($7,000) or a 25% fee on the forgiven amount ($8,000). In those cases, you would either pay $1,750 or $2,000 in fees to the debt settlement company in addition to the $7,000 or $8,000 you would have to pay to the lender. You may also have setup fees and maintenance fees for any accounts held with the debt settlement company during the process.

- **It's not a guarantee your debt will be settled:** Although debt settlement companies make hefty promises, they more often than not come up empty. Lenders will not easily accept to settle an account.

If you find yourself in a position where you are unable to make payments on your account for legitimate reasons, you may be able to contact your lender and make an attempt to settle your account on your own. Here's what you should do:

- Be ready to explain your situation to them and be prepared for them to ask for income verification and any documents supporting your reason(s) for not being able to make payments (hospital records, disability documents, etc.). Remember, they want to make sure you are legitimately unable to pay back your debt.

- Plan to offer them 30-35% of the settled amount initially, with the goal of eventually settling for 50%. Be sure to have 50% of the settled amount saved up already. Don't be surprised if they don't hop, skip, and jump to accept your offer. It may take several phone calls and speaking to several agents before any promising conversations begin.

- If they do agree to settle and accept less, make sure to get that in writing BEFORE making any payments. Do not provide them with any of your checking/savings account information.

- Lastly, check your credit history regularly to ensure all of your information is updated and accurate.

The Truth About Bankruptcy

Bankruptcy is a term you will likely hear at some point in your life. It's an option explored by individuals who find themselves in dire financial situations from job loss, disability, loss of a loved one, failed business, etc. Some make it seem like a quick fix to all of your debt problems, however, it could not be further from the truth. Bankruptcy is a serious matter with great financial implications. It is a legal process whereby a person declares him/herself or a business unable to pay back outstanding debts. During the legal proceeding, the judge examines your assets and liabilities to determine your ability to pay the debts. If it is determined that you are really unable to pay back your debts, the judge would discharge those debts and you would declare bankruptcy. Bankruptcy should be a last resort. It should not be considered until you have done everything in your power to become debt free. If you've exhausted all options (such as the steps listed in this book) and still find it difficult to keep your head above water, then you may feel like you have no other option but to pursue bankruptcy.

Important Things To Know

Certain debts are not eligible for bankruptcies. Those debts include student loans, government debt (taxes and fines), child support, alimony, and big-ticket items purchased right before filing for bankruptcy.

The two most common types of bankruptcy are *Chapter 7* and *Chapter 13*. Here's a quick snippet of what they each entail.

Chapter 7 Bankruptcy

In a Chapter 7 bankruptcy, you agree to liquidate (sell) all assets in order to pay back as much debt as possible to the lenders. This can include your home, car, or a company you own. The remaining amount of debt, if any, would be discharged after four months. The record of this type of bankruptcy would remain on your credit report for *ten years*. If you desire to keep your assets, then a Chapter 13 bankruptcy may be the better option.

Chapter 13 Bankruptcy

The Chapter 13 bankruptcy gives you the opportunity to pay back your debt over a three to five-year period via a repayment plan. With this type of bankruptcy, you are allowed to keep the assets you own and are given time to catch up with mortgage payments. You must follow a strict budget that is monitored closely by the court. The record of this type of bankruptcy stays on your credit report for *seven years*.

Filing for bankruptcy is not free. There are costs associated with the process and the prices may vary between the two options. An in depth look into bankruptcy is beyond the scope of this book. Please seek the assistance of a bankruptcy attorney for more specific details and counsel regarding the process. Again, bankruptcy should be a last resort after you have exhausted all other options to become debt free.

What <u>NOT</u> To Do On Your Debt-Free Journey

DO NOT GO FURTHER INTO DEBT

This should go without saying, but I will say it anyway. You should not go further into debt if your goal is to be debt free. You cannot continue the habits that landed you in the red. You must stop the bleeding. Do not spend more than you earn, stay away from credit cards, cease impulse buying, and learn to say no. Instead, stick to your zero-based budget and live below your means. You will not get far if you are constantly taking one step forward and two steps backward.

DO NOT COSIGN A LOAN

> *26Don't agree to guarantee another person's debt or put up security for someone else.*
> *27If you can't pay it, even your bed will be snatched from under you.*
> - Proverbs 22:26-27 NLT

If someone ever asks you to cosign a loan, run! No, seriously. You need to run! When you cosign a loan, you guarantee to pay a borrower's debt if he/she defaults on the loan. Cosigning a loan is commonplace in the world of lending. If someone has bad credit, they will have difficulty being approved for a loan. Typically, those individuals may be subject to higher interest rates and higher monthly payments and may be required to have a cosigner on the loan to increase their chances of approval. If you are the one in the family that seems to be the most financially responsible and has a good credit history, you may be the perfect candidate for them to ask. The request may come off as innocent. It may come from that favorite aunt of yours who just needs a little help to get that apartment. It may come from the cousin you grew up with who needs your help getting that new vehicle with a 10-15% interest rate. It may not seem like a big deal. After all, they are not asking you for money this time. All they are asking for is your name on a piece of paper. It's the least you can do, right? What's the harm in that? The risks are many.

You Are Responsible for the Entire Loan Amount

When you cosign a loan, you agree to pay back the borrower's full debt amount if he/she is unable to do so. That loan amount will be added to your current debt, thereby increasing your debt-to-income ratio. *This is essentially you taking on more debt.*

Your Credit Could Be Ruined

If the person you cosigned for defaults on his/her loans, you become liable for those loans as stated above. The loan you cosigned for will show up on your credit history as well as the borrower's. Therefore, any delinquent accounts will also appear there. The lenders will start coming after you to collect payments and your credit score could be ruined in the process.

You Are Married to the Loan

Once you cosign a loan, you cannot remove your name from that loan. You are under a legally binding agreement for the duration of the loan terms. To get your name removed, the person would have to refinance the loan to new terms but requalify on his/her own.

The dangers of cosigning a loan far outweigh the

benefits. The risks are too high. I know you may have a sincere and genuine desire to help that person, but there are other ways to help without signing your life away. One way you can help is by allocating a portion of your budget specifically for the purpose of helping relatives in desperate need. You can choose to do this on a monthly or quarterly basis, but be sure to establish clear boundaries so you are not enabling anyone. I know it may feel awkward to say no to cosigning a loan, but they will get over it and your relationship will be preserved for avoiding that trap. Remember, if someone asks you to cosign a loan, run and don't look back!

DO NOT BORROW MONEY TO PAY BACK DEBT

It seems like everywhere you turn lending institutions are offering you opportunities to borrow money. And, when you're drowning in debt, it can sometimes become appealing to take out a loan to pay back your debt. These loans come in the form of personal loans, payday loans, home equity loans/lines of credit, or even borrowing from a close friend or family member. It may be tempting to get a personal loan to pay off that credit card with a high-interest rate. You might even consider tapping into the equity in your home (meaning your home is worth more than the balance of your mortgage) to pay back your debt. Or, maybe you have an uncle you are really close to who may be willing to let you borrow some money. All of these options seem like they would solve your debt problems, but in reality they won't.

Home Equity Line of Credit and Home Equity Loan

By taking out a home equity line of credit or home equity loan, you are taking an unsecured debt (credit card) and turning it into a secured debt (home). In essence, you would now be putting your home at risk by using it as collateral in the event you defaulted on your loans. This is not a good idea.

Borrowing From Family Members

Borrowing from a loved one is not necessarily a better option either. It puts you at risk of ruining the relationship in case you cannot keep your word on paying it back. Confident that won't be an issue? I wouldn't be. There's a reason you're in this situation to begin with.

Using these options will not solve your debt problems. They are just ways to mask the underlying issue and make the situation you're in seem a bit less painful. *You do know you're not really paying off your debt by using another loan, right?* Focus on the root of the issue before you address the symptoms.

Retirement Accounts

It is never a good idea to cash out or borrow from your retirement accounts early to pay off debt. Some plans allow you to borrow from your 401k account (401k loan) and pay yourself back, however, that would be counterproductive as you would essentially be taking out one loan in order to pay off another. If you withdraw money before 59 ½ years of age (401k early withdrawal), you will be assessed a 10% early withdrawal penalty from the IRS. Additionally, you will have to pay income tax on the distribution amount based on your current tax bracket. That means the average middle-income family would be taxed at a 25% tax rate in addition to the 10% early withdrawal penalty. For example, let's say you have $20,000 in your retirement account and wanted to withdraw it. That would be the equivalent of you borrowing $20,000 at 35% interest to pay off your debt! For example, on a five-year loan, your minimum monthly payment would be $710 and the total amount of interest you would pay by the end of the term would be $22,588! So, let me phrase that in the form of a question. Would you borrow $20,000 with a 35% interest rate? I certainly would not! Instead, cash out all of your *non-retirement* accounts. Do everything you can, but DO NOT cash out your retirement accounts early to pay back debt.

Now that you have learned about the options above and have decided on a debt payoff method, it's time to transition to the execution part of attacking your debt.

Paying off debt is no easy task. If it were, the majority of people in debt would be aggressively paying theirs off. We all know this is not the case. Why? Because, the journey to debt freedom requires much more than people are willing to give: their comfort, toys, time, and money. To them, sacrificing is not as exciting as spending and discipline is not as tempting as diving deeper into debt. When you take a look at your life and your finances, can you honestly say you're in a good financial position? No, I am not asking if you can afford your monthly payments or if you have a good credit score. Think beyond that. Are you on course to leave generational wealth or generational debt? As higher income earners with more education and more opportunity than some of your parents had, how is it that you would leave your (future) children the same inheritance that was left for you? We should be passing down far more knowledge and assets to the generations after us! Something must change. You cannot continue to fund your lifestyle by borrowing/financing everything you want. You cannot continue to live above your means by spending more than you earn. The definition of insanity is doing the same thing over and over and expecting different results. You must make a conscious decision to get out of debt; you must be all in.

All In

Without commitment, you'll never get started.
But most importantly, without consistency
you'll never finish. - Denzel Washington

What does "be all in" look like? For us, *all in* meant sleeping apart from each other at night more than we slept together during our first year of marriage (Faith's side hustle was overnight nursing). *All in* meant 94-hour work weeks, at times, for Faith between her full-time job and side hustles. NINETY-FOUR hours in ONE week!

That's the equivalent of working more than two full-time jobs in one week! Let that sink in. *All in* for me meant working six days a week for 11 weeks in a row and signing up to work every Saturday and every major holiday. That meant long days, longer weeks, and less sleep. We literally had *hi* and *bye* kind of moments. For example, there were times when I would return home from my side hustle at the hospital and Faith would be getting ready to leave for her overnight nursing side hustle. When she would return the next morning from that overnight job, I would be leaving for my side hustle again. We were *all in*! Here's a snippet of what a typical work week was for Faith during our peak months of aggressively paying off debt.

Real Life Work Schedule

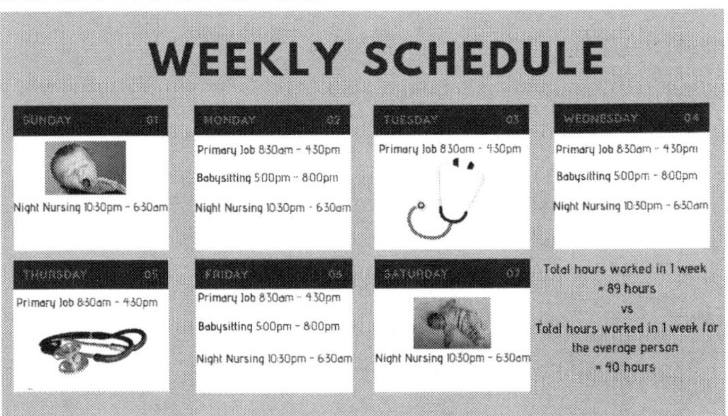

Figure 2.

Still not convinced we were *all in*? We packed the same lunches to work for months on end to cut our food expenses. *All in* meant cooking dinner at home and eating leftovers all week. It meant carpooling to work. It meant rotating between the same three pants and 6 polo shirts for work for over five years. It meant wearing shoes until there were holes in them and being forced only by the rain to buy new ones. It meant cutting cable and using an antenna for television. *All in.* That meant no vacation until 14 months after we started our journey and after we had worked our butts off to pay off over six figures of debt. We even delayed celebrating our one-year anniversary! It meant holding on to my five-year-old iPhone 5s for dear life because my monthly bill is less than $22/month. *All in.* That meant resisting the urge to swipe our cards when our flesh screamed "I WANT THIS." The word *no* began to flow freely from our lips. What was initially painful became easy to say, not only to ourselves, but to our families, friends, and each other. We were fighting for our freedom. We had to be *all in.*

Are you ready to go *all in*? Are you ready to stop playing *house* with your debt and finally give it its eviction notice? Your debt has been too comfortable for too long. It's time you kick it to the curb for good. Decrease your expenses, spend less than you make, and increase your income. Then take all of the money you've saved and earned and put it all toward your debt. That's the way to *ATTACK your debt*!

Set It Up. Then Knock It Out!

In boxing, the most important punch is the jab. You probably thought it was the hook, the uppercut, or some of the other power punches you've seen in knockout rounds. However, the jab, though it seems like a tap on the face compared to other punches, is actually more important. The reason for this is that it actually sets the opponent up to receive that knockout punch. Though they are seemingly small and seemingly less impactful, the intensity of the fight does not decrease when you're throwing jabs in boxing. In fact, throwing jabs creates constant pressure and little room for the opponent to gain ground. They keep the opponent off balance and puts them right where you want them. The jab doesn't end the fight, but it certainly sets up everything that does. Likewise, the journey to debt freedom is a fight. When you decrease your spending and throw that money at your debt, it's like throwing a jab. When you get a side hustle and put all of the money you've earned toward your debt, you're throwing a jab. You're setting it up for that final knockout punch. Are you ready to *ATTACK your debt?*

> *No discipline is enjoyable while it is happening—it's painful! But afterward, there will be a peaceful harvest of right living for those who are trained in this way. - Hebrews 12:11 NLT*

Stop buying things you don't need. Eat out less. Bring your own lunch to work. Cook dinner at home for the week. Dave Ramsey says, "beans and rice and rice and beans," but for you that may be peanut butter and jelly sandwiches and Ramen noodles. Well, you can make more appetizing meals than that, but cook on a budget! If you decrease your grocery bill by $20, throw it at your debt immediately. Learn to say *no*. Turning down the invite to go out with your friends isn't the coolest thing to do, but they will be just fine, and so will you. Remember that saying *no* does not necessarily mean you're saying *never*; it simply means *not now* and that's okay. Take the money you would have spent going out with your friends and put it toward your debt instead. Learn to silence the voice that tells you to spend on impulse. It does not control you. Be content with what you have. You don't need new clothes. You probably have more than enough shoes. If you do need new clothes, try shopping at the thrift store. When you save money in one category, it is not grounds for you to go out and spend it in another area. Like the old adage says, "don't rob Peter to pay Paul." Instead, put it toward your debt. Faith and I have been tempted on many occasions to use leftover money from one category and use it as discretionary spending, but we refrained. It's one of the non-negotiables we've disciplined ourselves to commit to on our journey. Even if it's just $5, put it toward your debt anyway. That $5 will add up and get you closer to debt freedom.

Hustle. Grind. Work.

When you've cut down as much spending as you possibly can, attack your debt by increasing your income. Then, put all of that money toward your debt. Pick up extra shifts at work. Get a side hustle or two. Work overtime. Work overnight. Work weekends and holidays. You must adapt the *by any means necessary* attitude. So what if you don't feel like getting up for your side hustle on a Saturday? Get up anyway. So what if you miss that event because you have to work an extra shift? There will be many more events like it when you're debt free. So what if you can't have that luxury car? You'll enjoy it more without a car note. At this point, it is no longer about your preferences, your feelings, or your convenience. This is about your freedom. There will be days when you will feel like nothing can stop you and other days when you feel defeated. There will be times you feel as motivated as ever and other times when you don't know if you can seriously continue. It is one roller coaster of a journey Do not expect everyone to be excited for you either. They may say it to your face with a smile but in their minds think you're crazy for embarking on such a journey. You may feel lonely at times and have moments when you feel like no one gets what you're going through. Don't worry. You will have the last laugh.

Now, let's look at some specific strategies you can implement to ATTACK your debt!

Strategies for Paying Off Debt

Automate Your Payments

Set up auto-pay for all of the loans you have with a lending institution. When you set your accounts up for auto-pay, you give the lender permission to automatically debit the minimum payments from your accounts every month on a specific date of your choosing. In turn, most lenders will reduce the interest rate on every account you have enrolled by 0.25%. For example, if you have a loan with an interest rate of 6.5%, your interest rate would be reduced to 6.25% while on auto-pay. Any amount helps!

Being enrolled in auto-pay will also ensure you don't miss any of your monthly payments.

Figure 3.

Make Extra Payments Toward Debt on PAYDAY

This strategy is particularly helpful for anyone who gets paid irregularly and lacks self-control or discipline. Paying off your debt as soon as you get paid will ensure you do not get tempted to use the money on anything other than the amount you planned in your budget to pay toward your debt. We started implementing this strategy when Faith's payday from her side hustle was different than our paydays from our full-time jobs. This strategy was necessary because the amount of pay we received from our side hustles varied depending on how many hours we worked. We actually got it down to a science. I called the lending institution and asked how long it would take for a payment to be processed and debited from our checking account. I was told it would take two business days and I confirmed this with several agents on separate occasions. I also asked what the cutoff time was for the end of the business day. So, when Faith's paycheck was scheduled to be deposited on a Friday during an off week, I would schedule an extra payment the Wednesday prior. By Friday morning, her paycheck was deposited into our checking account and the extra debt payment was being processed by the lending institution, leaving us no room to even consider spending that money on anything else. The money was already gone!

Stop Contributing to Your Retirement Accounts (401(k) and 403(b)) TEMPORARILY

For some people, this recommendation is really hard to commit to. The reason for this is the percentage match most employers give their employees for contributing to their retirement accounts. Why would I recommend you give up free money, one might ask? The answer is simple. You are giving the lending institutions free money by remaining in debt and accruing interest on your debt! Moreover, the interest on your loans is likely higher than the match you would be receiving from your employer. You did not think of that for this argument, did you? Except, the biggest difference is this - by paying off your debt, you get a guaranteed return on the money you pay off compared to the money given by your employers, which is subject to risk in your retirement account.

Now, I am not telling you to stop contributing to your retirement accounts forever. I only recommend you stop *temporarily* so all of your focus, energy, and money can be used to aggressively attack your debt. Remember this important fact: by following the 7 Bulletproof Steps written in this book, you should not be in debt for as long as many might think. Once you are debt free, you will be able to take all of the monthly payments you were using toward debt and allocate them toward your retirement accounts. This will result in an enormous amount of money going into your retirement accounts, if you so choose. Not only will you make up for lost time, it will seem like you never skipped a beat!

Use Your Refund Check (If You Get One) From Your Tax Return to Pay Off Your Debt

Believe it or not, many people look forward to tax filing season. Once the holidays are over, their attention is directed toward the pot of gold, known as the "refund check," they're accustomed to receiving every spring. They waste no time coming up with a "good" use for that money. Typically, it's for a summer vacation to Punta Cana or a cruise to the Bahamas. If you are one of those people who receive a refund check, I want you to use that money to pay off your debt instead. Yes, your entire refund check!

Deplete Your Savings Accounts (Except for Your Starter Emergency Fund) and Cash Out All Non-Retirement Accounts

In Chapter 6, we discussed the importance of having a starter emergency fund set aside before tackling your debt. While many people do not have an emergency fund, there are some who are faced with a different struggle. These individuals have a good amount of money in their savings, while also owing tons of debt and have not fully committed to being debt free. They choose to hoard their money rather than use it toward debt because the "what ifs" of the world seem to paralyze them from making the right decision. I struggled with this for a long time myself. I got into the habit of trying to grow our savings account even while in debt because I found a sense of security in knowing we had a good amount saved up. When Faith and I got married, we had a little over $21,000 in our savings account from money we had saved up individually and also from monetary wedding gifts. A month after we met with our CFP, she suggested we put $10,000 of it toward debt. At first, we hesitated and were reluctant at the thought of parting ways with it all at once! We had been saving for a long time to get to this point! However, we knew if we truly desired to be debt free, we would have to make radical decisions such as this one. The fact that we would have $11,000 left in our savings account certainly helped me cope with this. So, we decided to put $10,000 toward my student loans ($54,000 balance at the time) in August

2017 to start our journey and we knew there was no turning back. By the time December 2017 rolled around, we had a little over $12,000 in our account while the remaining balance of the student loans under my name was $11,051.17. Though we had enough to pay off the balance, I once again struggled to make that decision. The crazy part is that our money was earning less than 1% interest in our online savings account at the time, while the student loan debt was costing us far more with interest rates up to 6.8%! Long story short, I finally came to my senses and paid off that entire balance by using the money in our savings account. By making the decision to deplete our savings, less our $1,000 starter emergency fund, we paid off that loan 6 years faster and saved approximately $9,693.36 in the process!

Figure 4.

Some of you are in a similar position. You have a good amount saved up but are unwilling to put it toward your debt. I will pose the same question I asked in Chapter 6. How many of your emergencies in the past year eclipsed the recommended starter emergency fund amount? I know your concerns are legitimate ones, but keeping all of that money in your account is costing you far more than you think. For these reasons, I recommend you cash out all non-retirement accounts, less your starter emergency fund, so you can make a huge dent in paying off your balance. That includes cashing out CDs, mutual funds, whole life policies, savings accounts, bonds, etc. It will be one of the best decisions you make on your journey!

INSIDE SCOOP

When we started our debt-free journey, Faith also cashed out a little over $10,000 in bonds that were given to her as a child by her grandfather and mother. We didn't go on a vacation with this unexpected blessing. You're probably thinking, "But surely a surprise like this should be enjoyed and not swallowed into debt?" Wrong! We put it all toward our debt! If you're committed to living in freedom, your perspective is different, and the sacrifices *are small compared to the end goal. This is yet another way we were able to accelerate our debt payoff timeline!*

Use the Extra (Third or Fifth) Paycheck You Receive and Apply It Toward Your Debt

If you're an employee who gets paid bi-weekly, there are two months out of the year when you receive three paychecks in one month! If you get paid weekly, there are several times during the course of the year when you will receive a fifth paycheck. Yes, you read that correctly. Have you not noticed this? This occurs because the fifty-two weeks in the year are not distributed evenly. Because many of your expenses are paid on a monthly basis, during those months you will end up with some extra cash. Guess what I advise you to do? You guessed it! I want you to allocate it toward your debt! Of course, during those longer months, you may have increased expenses (an extra week for groceries to consider, for example), but I want you to plan for this ahead of time in your budget.

Here's a quick list showing which months contain five weeks from the year 2019 to 2025 for those who get paid weekly:

- **2019:** March, May, August, November
- **2020:** January, May, July, October
- **2021:** January, April, July, October, December
- **2022:** April, July, September, December

- **2023:** March, June, September, December
- **2024:** March, May, August, November
- **2025:** January, May, August, November

Now that you know this little nugget, I want you to use that extra cash to fast-track your debt payoff goals!

Use Any Bonus or Raise You Receive and Apply It Toward Your Debt

In BULLETPROOF STEP 5 – *Decrease Expenses + Increase Income*, I discussed the importance of avoiding lifestyle creep. This is the concept of fighting the temptation to spend more just because you are earning more. Instead, you should use all of the money you receive from a bonus or a raise to pay off your debt faster! Once you are debt free, you can use that money to grow your wealth!

Loan Repayment Programs

The federal government and a few other organizations have developed loan repayment programs (LRPs) for certain high-demand health professions as a way to incentivize professionals in those fields to work in underserved communities. The LRPs offer student loan repayment assistance for individuals who commit to a period of service (typically 2 years) in a critical shortage area. The value amount of the awards may vary between organizations. This is the perfect opportunity to pay off your debt faster if you meet the criteria and don't mind making the service commitment. Here are a few LRPs to look into.

National Health Service Corps (NHSC) Loan Repayment Program (LRP)

> The NHSC LRP is administered by the Health Resources and Services Administration (HRSA) of the U.S. Department of Health and Human Services (HHS). The NHSC LRP seeks primary care physicians, nurse practitioners, certified nurse-midwives, physician assistants, dentists, dental hygienists, and behavioral and mental health providers (psychiatrists, health service psychologists, licensed clinical social workers, marriage and family therapists, psychiatric nurse specialists, and licensed professional counselors) to provide culturally competent, interdisciplinary primary health care services to underserved populations. *The program will pay up to $50,000 for a two-year commitment. NHSC Loan Repayment funds are exempt from federal income and employment taxes.* This organization also offers scholarships to certain health professions students.[7]

The Nurse Corps Loan Repayment Program (LRP)

Nurse Corps LRP offers loan repayment for nurses who practice at health care facilities with a critical shortage of nurses. For two years of service, the program offers to pay *60 percent of your eligible student debt.* You can also extend service for another year and receive an additional

25 percent. This program also offers scholarships for nursing students who agree to practice in areas with limited access to care.[8] This is the scholarship Faith received that paid for her Master of Science in Nursing program at Emory University.

The National Institutes of Health Loan Repayment Program

> The NIH Loan Repayment Programs (LRPs) are a set of programs established by Congress and designed to recruit and retain highly qualified health professionals into biomedical or biobehavioral research careers. The LRPs repay up to *$35,000 annually* (or a *maximum of $70,000 for a two-year award*) of a researcher's qualified educational debt in return for a commitment to engage in NIH mission-relevant research. There are eight LRPs, five for researchers not employed by NIH (Extramural) and three for researchers employed by NIH (Intramural).[9]

There are many more of these types of programs at the state level. Contact your state professional organization to learn of more opportunities that may be available to you.

Tips for College Students and New Graduates

Most students are never fully informed of the financial implications of attending college. We learn how to borrow money through FAFSA, but we don't hear much about the loans we borrowed until it's time to graduate four years later. This reality leaves college students and new graduates at a significant disadvantage. Below are a few tips I strongly recommend and wish I knew or took heed of as it pertains to navigating college with student loan debt.

Apply for Work Study or Get a Job Off Campus

Federal work-study is a federally funded program in the U.S. that provides part-time jobs to college and graduate students with financial need. This program allows those students to earn money to pay for some of their educational expenses. In college, I worked as a staff at the campus gym for three-hour shifts a few days per week. I also worked as a mail sorter in my dormitory. If you do not qualify for work-study, you can search for a job off campus such as babysitting or working at a nearby restaurant on the weekends. By earning income through a part-time job, you would not have to take out as much in loans and you can begin to pay the interest on your student loans while in school.

Pay Interest on Your Student Loans While in College

Paying off the interest on my student loans while in college was one of the best pieces of advice I received as an undergraduate student. I remember exactly where I was when I was told this valuable information. I was working part-time at K&G Fashion Superstore in the mall during my sophomore year of college. One day during lunch my manager saw me leaving Best Buy, which was located next to our store. I told him I was looking to purchase a digital camera for my upcoming trip to Haiti. When I shared how much the camera cost, my manager suggested that I use the money to pay off the interest on my student loans instead of making such a big purchase. I nodded as I listened to him explain the reasoning behind the recommendation at the front register. However, like most college students, I purchased the $300 Canon digital camera anyway and never paid anything toward interest while I was in college (despite working throughout college and graduate school). Now that I understand the effects of compounding interest and the enormous amount of interest you can accrue on your loans over time, I would strongly encourage you to pay toward your interest while in college. Even payments of $50/month would go a long way. Please don't do what I did. Heed my advice. You'll be happy you made that small sacrifice when the 6-month grace period on your student loans comes to an end!

"Refund" Check

The "refund" check isn't actually a refund. It is money you borrowed in excess of what you actually needed to cover the cost of tuition, room and board, and supplies. The loan provider gives you the leftover amount in the form of a "refund" check and most students think of it as free money for them to spend. I sure did! I remember the long lines of peers joyously waiting in the Bursar's office to receive their checks. What most students don't realize is this: the money from the "refund" check will have to be repaid along with the remainder of their student loans once they graduate. Not only will they have to pay it back, but the sum of money from the check is also accruing interest the entire time until it is repaid! If you happen to receive a "refund" check, I would strongly recommend you return it to the lending institution. If your refund check was $1,000, that would be $1,000 plus interest accumulated over the years that you would not have to pay back once you graduate. I know it may be tempting to keep it and splurge, but remember this simple truth: the "refund" check isn't actually a refund.

Scholarships

We have all been told to apply for scholarships before starting college or graduate school in order to help cover the cost of tuition. The mistake most students make is that they stop applying once they start their freshman year. But did you know you can continue to apply for scholarships while in school? In fact, some of the awards are only available for those who are already in school. Because scholarships have different due dates, I would recommend you make it a routine to check for scholarships every semester. Make a list of the scholarships you qualify for, including all of their respective deadlines. The more scholarships you receive, the less you would have to take out in loans. As stated previously, here are two great resources I recommend you look into for scholarship opportunities:

- The Ultimate Scholarship Book 2019 on Amazon
- Myscholly.com

Avoid Lifestyle Creep

I mentioned avoiding lifestyle creep as a recommendation in Chapter 7 – BULLETPROOF STEP 5 in the section on increasing income. Lifestyle creep is the tendency of individuals to increase their spending when their income increases. Well, an income increase is what you expect as a new graduate, right? Absolutely! As a new graduate starting your career, you will be earning substantially more than what you were earning while in school. That's a great thing. However, I do not want you to increase your way of living substantially once you graduate. That's what most new graduates do as soon as they start earning more money. They buy a new car and start spending all of their money. They have no real plan for their finances and hold on to their debt for a long time, paying way more in interest than they have to. I want you to be different. If you need a car, purchase one for $5,000-$7,500 and pay cash for it. I want you to continue to sacrifice and live below your means. You should already be familiar with that lifestyle. I know, it wasn't the best. I only recommend you do this temporarily while you aggressively attack your debt. You will be in a much better position financially by addressing your debt sooner rather than later.

Live With Your Parents or Relatives Once You Graduate

I probably lost a few of you with this suggestion. I am also aware that this may not be an option for some people. However, if you are a new grad who has the option to live with a parent or relative for a short period of time after graduating, I would strongly recommend it. By doing this, you could save some money and get a head start on paying off your debt. Of course, I don't want you to free-load off of your parents. Come to an agreement with them. Offer to pay a few bills such as the electric bill or the internet bill. You can even offer to contribute to groceries. Make an agreement to pay a total of a few hundred bucks per month. This would be much less than what you would have to pay if you lived on your own. I know this may not be what you had in mind for when you graduated, but remember this would only be a temporary living situation. Living with your parents/relatives would enable you to put a dent in your debt balance at a much faster rate than you otherwise would be able to.

Are you still struggling with your commitment to attack your debt? Are you questioning your ability to reach your freedom goal?

Remember Why You Started. Remember Your Dream(s).

Start strong, stay strong, and finish strong by always remembering why you're doing it in the first place. – Ralph Marston

Remember your dreams from BULLETPROOF STEP 1? This is the perfect time to read over them again. Write them on sticky notes and post them on your bathroom mirror, on the dashboard of your car, and on your desk at work. This is the reason you started the journey in the first place. Are they important enough to make you take action? Who is depending on you to make this lifestyle change? Your spouse? Your children? Your future self? Will you leave those counting on you disappointed? Will you leave them thinking you loved your stuff more than you loved them? A debt-free life gives you options you may not have had before. By paying off your debt, you could have more money and flexibility in your budget, retire earlier, have a better mental health by reducing the stress in your life, work on your own terms, travel more, and give more. The best part about it is that you would no longer be at the mercies of the lending institutions! Wouldn't you rather spend your hard-earned money on yourself and the people and experiences that matter most to you? When will you finally realize your debt is enslaving you? Will you allow it to continue to cost you your freedom? I hope your answer to this last question is a resounding no! You will be debt free. Allow this mantra (war cry) to be a constant reminder and motivator for you on your journey to debt freedom.

DEBT-FREE MANTRA (WAR CRY)

My debt does not define who I am.
I forgive myself for all of my past financial mistakes.
I own up to them and take full responsibility for where I am now.
I make the vow to address them and move forward with better money decisions.
My debt is costing me my freedom and today is the day I say enough is enough.
I take control of my finances.
I have what it takes.
I am willing.
I will be debt free.

INSIDE SCOOP

If Faith and I continued to pay the minimum payments on our $211,000+ loans, it would have taken us 15 years to pay it off and it would have cost us $125,000 in interest alone. By aggressively paying off our debt using these 7 proven steps, it will take us less than 3 years and cost us approximately $26,000 in interest.

Before we continue, let me take the time to address mortgage debt for those of you whose only remaining debt is your mortgage. Remember, paying your mortgage off early is recommended only after you have addressed all other consumer debt and after other important milestones are in place.

Mortgage Debt

If you are reading this book and your only debt is your mortgage, congratulations! You are doing better than most! If you are simply wondering how to pay off your mortgage early once you are done paying off all non-mortgage debt, I will address your curiosity in this section. As stated in Chapter 7 titled "Step 5 - Decrease Expenses + Increase Income," your monthly mortgage payment should be 25-28% or less of your monthly take-home pay on a 15-year loan. If your home is on a 30-year loan, you should either pay it as if it were on a 15-year loan or look into refinancing it into a 15-year loan. This is one way to pay off your mortgage faster and save thousands in interest. Be advised that this will increase your monthly mortgage payments. Choosing to pay off your mortgage as if it were on a 15-year loan will only work if you are disciplined enough not to compromise on that commitment. What happens more often than not is that people will easily stop paying that additional amount as soon as an inconvenience occurs. Because the additional amount is technically not due and does not show up on the billing statement, it's easy to become lackadaisical and miss those extra payments here and there. Don't let that happen to you!

The following must be in place before I recommend you start paying your mortgage off early:

- All non-mortgage debt must be paid off.
- Monthly mortgage payments must be 25-28% or less of your monthly take-home pay on a 15-year loan.
- You should have a 3-6 month or 6-9-month emergency fund set aside.
- You should start investing 15-20% of your income for retirement.
- If you have children, you should start saving for a college/legacy fund.

Once those five milestones are in place, you are ready to start attacking your mortgage. Because your mortgage balance is one lump sum, there is no need for a debt snowball method or a debt avalanche method. However, you can implement some of the strategies I recommended earlier for paying off non-mortgage debt, such as living on a strict budget, decreasing your expenses, and increasing your income via side hustles. You would then do the exact same thing you did with the additional income you were able to free up or earn and put it directly toward your debt!

Some specific strategies for paying off your mortgage early include paying your mortgage bi-weekly or weekly instead of monthly (if your mortgage lender allows). To accelerate your goals even more, you can make an extra mortgage payment each year, or better yet, each quarter if you can! A good way to make extra payments if you don't have a lump sum of money is to divide your monthly principal and interest payment by 12 and add that amount as an extra payment to each monthly mortgage payment. This is known as the 1/12 Rule. This is how it would work if your monthly mortgage payment was $1,200.

- Divide $1,200 by 12 to obtain your extra payment amount for each month.
    - $1200/12 = 100
- Add $100 to your monthly mortgage payment.
    - $1,200 + $100 = $1,300
- An extra payment of $100 each month will result in one extra mortgage payment by the end of the year.

In essence, you would have made 13 payments in 12 months! Be sure to allocate your extra payments as *additional principal-only* payments and not as an early prepayment for the following month.

You may have the greatest intentions and the best plan of attack in the world to pay off your debt, however, that may not stop you from being pleasantly interrupted by some of life's most precious moments. Here's what I recommend you do to prepare if you are getting married and/or having a baby while on your debt-free journey.

Planning to Get Married While in Debt?

Planning to get engaged or get married while on your debt-free journey? Congratulations! This is a very exciting time for you! Being in debt should not stop you from transitioning into this beautiful chapter of your life. At the same time, getting engaged/married should not cause you to go further into debt. There are many factors to consider when planning, and of course, one size doesn't fit all. Here are a few helpful tips.

- Purchase a *budget-friendly* ring.

    Rings are typically expensive and can cost over $1,000 on average. The cost is obviously more for a man who needs to purchase both the engagement ring and the wedding band. My advice is for you to purchase a budget-friendly ring. Please have a conversation with your significant other *first* and come to an agreement on a price point for that budget-friendly ring. The last thing you want is for her to say no after seeing the ring! All jokes aside, buy something nice. However, there's no need to go over the top while in debt. You can always upgrade once you become debt free!

- Include saving for the ring as part of your *sinking fund.*

    Establishing a sinking fund, as discussed in the chapter on budgeting, is the perfect way to save for big-ticket items like a ring. Price the ring you like and set money aside every month until it's time to make the purchase. This way, purchasing a big-ticket item won't hurt as much. For more on sinking funds and how they work, please reference the section on it in Chapter 5.

- Budget for *a small* wedding and pay *cash* for it.

   There's always an urge to have a big wedding when you first start wedding planning. You start to think of all the people you need to invite: family members, extended family members, friends, co-workers, your childhood best friend you haven't spoken to in 10 years, your college classmate because they invited you to their wedding a couple of years ago, and the list goes on. One of the biggest wedding expenses is the amount you pay per plate for dinner at the reception. The truth is, everyone and their mother doesn't need to attend your wedding. A good general rule of thumb for narrowing your list down is to remove anyone on your list you haven't spoken to in a year or nine months. Plan to cash flow a wedding that is less than $10,000, even if your parents can afford to help out. Let them know of your plan to be debt free and use monetary gifts to pay off your debts!

- Stop making *extra* debt payments *temporarily IF* your wedding is *one year or less away.*

   If you plan to get married within the next year, you

should stop making extra debt payments temporarily and save as much and as fast as you can for your small wedding. If your wedding is more than one year away, move your wedding date up so you can start implementing this strategy. You definitely don't want to stop your accelerated debt payoff plan for longer than a year. Plus, if you know this is the person you want to marry, why are you waiting so long to tie the knot? You can also include saving for the wedding as part of your sinking fund.

What To Do If You Find Out You're Pregnant Or Desire To Be?

You're pregnant!! Congratulations!! You are probably experiencing a whirlwind of emotions at the thought of bringing new life into the world. Enjoy this moment and the process that lies ahead. If you're not yet pregnant and are wondering if you should wait until you are debt free to have a baby with your spouse, the answer is no. Being in debt should not prevent you from experiencing one of life's most precious moments! Having a baby is a gift from God. If you find yourself being pregnant or wanting to grow your family, below are a few strategies you can begin to implement today to prepare accordingly!

- STOP making *extra* debt payments (but continue to make minimum payments) once you find out you're pregnant. You will do this until mom and baby are back home safe and sound. This is advice I've heard from Dave Ramsey and I totally agree with it! You will accrue interest on your loans during that time, but that's better than not having enough money to cover your hospital expenses or any medical emergencies. Once mom and baby are home, take all of the money you did not use and put it all toward your debt.

- Call the billing office of the hospital to get an estimate of the total charges for labor and delivery.

- Call the OB-GYN office to get an estimate of the total charges for prenatal care and labor and delivery (compare it with what the hospital says).

- Continue to hustle (especially dads) to pile up as much cash as you possibly can to cover all of the estimated expenses for prenatal care (ultrasounds, birthing classes, prenatal vitamins, etc.) and labor and delivery.

- Have a good understanding of your healthcare coverage, including out-of-pocket costs such as deductibles, co-pays, and co-insurance.

- Call your health insurance company to make sure your OB-GYN doctors, anesthesiologist, and the hospital you plan to deliver at are all in network.

- Avoid getting unnecessary labs. As a new parent, you might feel the urge to get every test and lab mentioned to you during your prenatal visits. This may include tests for potential birth defects and genetic conditions, such as Down Syndrome. However, unless you have reason to suspect such conditions, these tests are not necessary and may not be covered by your insurance. You might be stuck with an expensive bill that gets you further into debt!

- Set money aside in a health savings account (HSA) or flexible spending account (FSA) through your employer if you have access to them. By doing this, you can save for your planned expenses using pre-tax dollars. Keep in mind that you must use the money in your FSA account by the end of the calendar year, however, you can use the money in your HSA account for qualified medical expenses at any time.

- Always ask if a service, product, or test is covered by your insurance before agreeing to anything.

While doing all that you possibly can to eradicate your debt, you will need a way to measure your progress and stay motivated on your journey. This is exactly why we created the Freedom Meter.

Freedom Meter

The Freedom Meter is the poster Faith and I use to track the progress we make on paying off our debt. Because we had so much success with it, we designed one specifically to help you visually track your progress as well! We have all heard how important it is to write your goals down.

Research shows that people who write their goals down are significantly more likely to achieve them compared to those who don't. What research also shows is the power of visual information in goal setting. Our brains have the ability to process 36,000 images per minute. It is estimated that 80-90% of the information received by the brain comes through the eyes.[10] Faith was on to something. She came up with the idea of a visual as soon as we started our journey to debt freedom. She wanted a way to visually see the progress we were making on paying off our loans. Remember the psychological and emotional factor I mentioned earlier in the chapter when discussing the debt snowball method? Well, adding a visual element to goal setting is yet another way to augment your chances of accomplishing your goals! There is a psychological and emotional connection that is established when a text is accompanied by a visual compared to when it stands alone as a text. And, anything that can address the emotional being of the person in a positive way during the journey to debt freedom is likely to increase the person's chances of actually paying off all of his/her debts. That's what the Freedom Meter did for us!

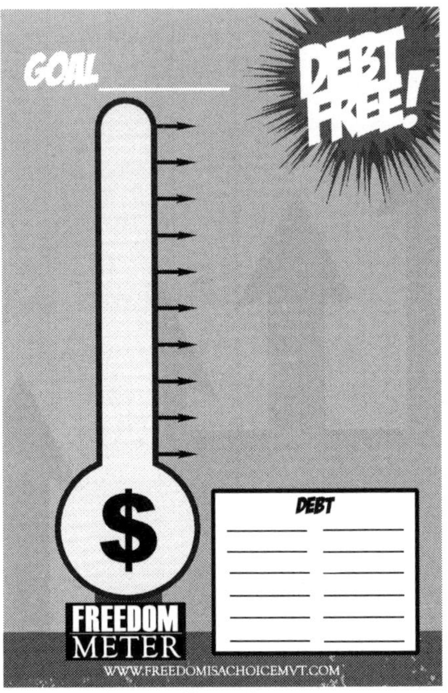

Figure 5.

Having the Freedom Meter has definitely been a huge part of our journey. It gives us something to feel good about and something we can both work on together. It's akin to seeing your penny jar gradually fill up over time. Just as a child would look forward to adding to their money jar and seeing it full one day, we look forward to paying off each debt and meeting our overall goal to pay off over $211,000 of debt!

Here's a quick snippet of how the Freedom Meter works. We write our total debt amount (our debt-free goal amount aka our target number) as our goal at the top. We then list all of our debts (the text component) in the box titled *debt* at the bottom right. Once we pay off a debt, we cross it off the list then color in our Freedom Meter (the thermometer) up until the last amount that was paid (the visual component). It's been really fun and exciting to visually see how far we've come along since we started. It has given us a great boost of motivation to continue working hard as we cannot wait for the day we get to cross off that last debt and color in the thermometer to the very top! If you are motivated to become debt free and need a fun and easy way to track the progress you're making on paying off your loans, this Freedom Meter is for you! Get yours today at www.freedomisachoicemvt.com.

Celebrations and Milestones

We consider any debt paid off a cause for celebration! Regardless of the amount of debt paid, we believe it's important for you to reward yourself for remaining on track with your goals. So, treat yourself! Does this mean you get to go splurge on all of your heart's desires? No. You're still in debt, you're still on a budget, and the plan to become debt free has not changed. However, you can celebrate within reason. Just make sure you plan for it in your budget. Celebrating can be as simple as going to the movies or getting your nails done. My wife and I are pretty simple people, so we don't require much. Most of the celebrations we've had from paying off our debts have consisted of treating ourselves to ice cream and by ordering pizza or Chinese! We love to eat!

You can also establish milestones on your journey to debt freedom. For example, you can set your milestones at $5,000 increments. Whenever you reach the $5,000, $10,000, $15,000 mark and so forth, you can do something a bit more special (but on a budget) as a way to reward yourself for all of your hard work and sacrifice. This will further increase your confidence in the process and motivate you to continue to ATTACK your debt. The debt snowball method gives you the opportunity to gain quick victories on those smaller debts. The purpose of this section is to give you permission to celebrate them. Cheers!

The Journey To Debt Freedom Is A Marathon, Not A Sprint!

The Summer Olympics is one of the largest events in the world. One of my favorite sporting events to watch is track and field. Most people tend to gravitate toward the sprinting events. They are more exciting and they are over before you can blink twice, leaving you in awe at what you just saw. But have you ever watched the long distance races such as the 5000m or the 10000m? In those events, there is a stark contrast. You would never see the long-distance runners expending all of their energy at the beginning of the race. They pace themselves. If they sprint in the beginning, they will run out of gas and compromise their chances of winning. Their race is entirely different. Even the fastest man in history, Usain Bolt, knows he can only maintain his lightning speed for so long. Likewise, you must know what race you're in and stay in your lane. The journey to debt freedom is a marathon, not a sprint.

Because the journey to debt freedom is a long and often grueling one, we encourage individuals and families to pace themselves by taking mini-breaks. Faith and I did a terrible job at this during our first year of attacking our debt. We hit the ground running as soon as we returned from our honeymoon and did not take a break until over a year later. Faith took a short break in June 2018 after we hustled our way to paying off over $104,000 of debt in 12 months. She had been working 80+ hours/week for months and was exhausted, out of steam, sleep deprived, you name it. She took a mini-break while I continued to work 6 days/week. We were finally able to take a real vacation 14 months after we started our journey. One of the biggest lessons I have learned over the past year is how important it is to take time to pause and recharge. It's not that we didn't want a break. We did. We even had the paid time off (PTO) from work to take breaks. It was a matter of not having the money to do so because we were literally using all of it to pay off our debt. I personally take the blame for this. In my mind, I thought there was no point in taking a break since we didn't have any money left over to enjoy. I was wrong. Working as much as we worked and for as long as we worked without any breaks not only put a toll on our bodies but on our marriage. We were stressed. We became irritable and easily annoyed with one another. Our responses were short and not the nicest at times. The times we didn't spend arguing were spent sleeping because we were exhausted. It wasn't healthy at all! However, when we finally took a break, we immediately noticed a shift. We were happier, less stressed, clear-minded, playful, the humor returned, and we were more engaging and loving toward one another. We were basically back to normal, I'd say! We decided from that point forward to take more consistent breaks for the health of our marriage, mind, body, and soul.

We encourage you to do the same. Your break does not have to be extravagant. You do not have to go anywhere fancy. It can be a short road trip to a nearby city/state or a staycation at home or at a local bed and breakfast. Take a weekend off from your side hustle, binge watch your favorite TV shows (Faith relaxes by watching Grey's Anatomy), sleep (my personal favorite), or pick up a book. It doesn't matter how you choose to take your breaks, as long as you take one (and, of course, cash flow it). The purpose of this is to give your mind and body a chance to recover. This will be an opportunity for you to de-stress, recharge, and reconnect with your loved ones. Be intentional about it and plan ahead. Know your limits and schedule time to rest before you hit your breaking point. You will be able to endure this marathon of a journey much better by pacing yourself. Most importantly, it will ensure you are re-energized when you return to ATTACK your debt!

The Road Less Traveled

The journey to debt freedom is a road less traveled. Many desire freedom, but few ever find it. This journey calls you out of your comfort zone and stretches you far beyond what you could ever imagine. It is by far one of the most difficult yet rewarding goals you could endeavor to pursue. But in light of the many years, God willing, you have ahead, it is only a season. It's a temporary sacrifice for a long-term gain. And in light of what's at stake, it is definitely worth it. So, do what you can with what you have. Do not compare yourself to others. Your journey will not look the same. With each payment you make, you regain control of your finances. With each debt you pay off, you begin to remove the chains that kept you in bondage all of these years. The Bulletproof Steps written in this book were created to bring you to this very moment – the moment you submit your final debt payment and walk into freedom.

Critical Thinking Questions

1. The title of this chapter is "STEP 6: ATTACK YOUR DEBT" and the subtitle is *Show No Mercy*. Why do you think we used this specific wording to describe this step?

2. What does *showing no mercy* toward your debt look like for you and your family?

The BULLETPROOF Steps in Review

STEP 1: DREAM

Establish your reason(s) for wanting to be debt free. This is the *why* behind the *what*. Your DREAM is the reason you start your journey, the reason you do not quit, the reason your spouse gets on board, and so much more! This is the first step toward debt freedom.

STEP 2: KNOW HOW MUCH YOU OWE

Identify your target number. This is your debt-free goal amount. List all of the lending institutions you owe, along with the current balance and interest rates for each loan. You cannot effectively strategize unless you know the exact amount you're up against.

STEP 3: BUDGET

Create a plan for your money. Give each dollar you earn

an *assignment* before you ever receive your paycheck. This way, all of your money is accounted for and not one penny is falling through the cracks. The formula is simple: Earn an income, prioritize by telling your money where it goes, and stick to your plan.

STEP 4: STARTER EMERGENCY FUND

Establish a starter emergency fund as a layer of protection and buffer against life's unexpected events as you diligently execute a plan to pay off your debt. This will ensure you remain on track on your journey and do not get further into debt. Emergencies will happen, but you do not have to be unprepared.

STEP 5: DECREASE EXPENSES + INCREASE INCOME

Spend less than you earn. Cut back on everything that is eating away at your budget. Create new income streams to generate more cash. Decreasing your expenses and increasing your income are two surefire ways to maximize cash flow and accelerate your debt payoff goals.

STEP 6: ATTACK YOUR DEBT

Create and execute a plan to ATTACK your debt. Be laser focused. Show no mercy. Your debt is your enemy. Do everything in your power to eliminate it once and for all. By any means necessary.

Chapter 9
STEP 7: FREEDOM
Sweet Victory

The period from 1791-1804 marked the Haitian Revolution, known as one of the largest and most successful slave rebellions in the Western Hemisphere. On January 1, 1804, Haiti became the first independent black republic in the world and the second nation (after the United States) to win its independence in the Americas. After their sweet victory, the Haitian slaves celebrated by eating soup joumou, a savory pumpkin soup that was once prohibited by their former French slave masters.

AHH!! YOU'RE HERE! You thought you would never make it, but I knew you would. Your dreams were far too great to allow them to be buried with you in the grave. Your legacy was far too important for you to not intentionally seek to impact future generations. I know you must be tired. It's been a long journey. Here, have a seat. Kick your feet up. It's totally okay. You've earned it. Help yourself to a glass of water and enjoy the view. Breathe. Can't you see? Everything is a bit different on this side. Just soak it all in. A world of opportunity awaits you. Welcome to freedom.

Why It Was So Important for You to Get to This Point

- Being debt free gives you options you did not have before.
- You are now unrestrained (by finances) to pursue your dreams.
- Your money can now be used toward your future instead of your past.
- Better mental health is possible without the added burden of debt.
- You can now improve your quality of life.
- Money used to pay off debt can now be used to grow your wealth.
- You can become financially independent and retire early.
- You can live life on your own terms.
- You have the opportunity to pass down generational wealth and leave a lasting legacy.
- You are no longer enslaved to the lending institutions.

- Worry, stress, and fear about finances are significantly reduced.
- You are better able to set your kids up for success.
- You no longer have to live paycheck to paycheck.
- You are able to be generous with your giving.
- You are more equipped to withstand emergencies and inconveniences.
- Your broke days are over.

Your Broke Days Are Over

It probably hasn't dawned on you yet, but you are debt free!!!! Say it out loud with me. Matter of fact, scream it out loud! Ready? Go! "I'm debt free!!!" Most adults will never be able to say that. Isn't that sad? However, that is not your story anymore. Now that you've paid off your debt, you can have a positive net worth for once in your life. Or maybe your net worth is $0. Guess what? That's still better than most Americans! Yikes! Does this mean you can now go buy that luxury car you always wanted or the new $350 YEEZY sneakers? You can. However, just because you can, it does not mean you should. Now that you are out of debt, it is time to do everything in your power to stay out of it for good! This is not the time to go back to your old spending habits and swipe on impulse. That's the reason you got into debt in the first place – poor financial behavior. There should be no more living from paycheck to paycheck. There should be no more borrowing/financing.

You no longer have to succumb to the pressure to live like everyone else. Believe it or not, you are where they want to be – debt free! When the season comes to spend money and buy things again, pay cash; cash is king! Yes, even if it is for a car. It's time to build upon the money habits you developed on your journey to debt freedom: budgeting, discipline, contentment, frugality. Continue to live below your means by spending less than you earn. Be intentional. Be a better steward of your finances. Your broke days are over. However, there's still work to be done. It's time to pass down generational wealth and build a lasting legacy.

Full Circle

Your goal to be debt free started with a dream. That was your reason for enduring this journey. Now that you are debt free, your dream(s) can actually become a reality. Was your dream to start a business? Was it to give generously to others? Was it to be able to pay for private school for your children? Whatever your dreams are, I'm here to let you know they are possible. Now is when you can begin to build upon the foundation you laid by achieving this important financial milestone. You can start to change your family tree. You can be the catalyst that impacts even your children's children. This is where you would fully fund your emergency fund, start investing, save up for a home, and so much more! Maybe I'll write another book to discuss these financial building blocks in more detail. For now, I want you to enjoy the fruit of your labor. Celebrate! Take that long-awaited vacation. Order yourself a Charbroiled Kobe Filet. Freedom is a choice and I am so glad you chose freedom. It's already looking good on you!

DEBT-FREE MANTRA (WAR CRY)

My debt does not define who I am.
I forgive myself for all of my past financial mistakes.
I own up to them and take full responsibility for where I am now.
I make the vow to address them and move forward with better money decisions.
My debt is costing me my freedom and today is the day I say enough is enough.
I take control of my finances.
I have what it takes.
I am willing.
I will be debt free.

Critical Thinking Questions

1. January 1st is Haiti's Independence Day and on this day Haitians all over the world eat soup joumou as a way to celebrate and commemorate their independence. What are some things you would be able to do if you were debt free?
2. What are some ways you plan to celebrate once you become debt free?

The BULLETPROOF Steps in Review

STEP 1: DREAM

Establish your reason(s) for wanting to be debt free. This is the *why* behind the *what*. Your DREAM is the reason you start your journey, the reason you do not quit, the reason your spouse gets on board, and so much more! This is the first step toward debt freedom.

STEP 2: KNOW HOW MUCH YOU OWE

Identify your target number. This is your debt-free goal amount. List all of the lending institutions you owe, along with the current balance and interest rates for each loan. You cannot effectively strategize unless you know the exact amount you're up against.

STEP 3: BUDGET

Create a plan for your money. Give each dollar you earn an *assignment* before you ever receive your paycheck. This way, all of your money is accounted for and not one penny is falling through the cracks. The formula is simple: Earn an income, prioritize by telling your money where it goes, and stick to your plan.

STEP 4: STARTER EMERGENCY FUND

Establish a starter emergency fund as a layer of protection and buffer against life's unexpected events as you diligently execute a plan to pay off your debt. This will ensure you remain on track on your journey and do not get further into debt. Emergencies will happen, but you do not have to be unprepared.

STEP 5: DECREASE EXPENSES + INCREASE INCOME

Spend less than you earn. Cut back on everything that is eating away at your budget. Create new income streams to generate more cash. Decreasing your expenses and increasing your income are two surefire ways to maximize cash flow and accelerate your debt payoff goals.

STEP 6: ATTACK YOUR DEBT

Create and execute a plan to ATTACK your debt. Be laser focused. Show no mercy. Your debt is your enemy. Do everything in your power to eliminate it once and for all. By any means necessary.

STEP 7: FREEDOM

Live life on your own terms! Become so financially secure and stable you forgot it was payday. Build wealth. Leave a legacy that changes your family tree. So much more is possible when you are debt free!

NOTES

Chapter 1: CONTACT LEFT, 9 O'CLOCK... MULTIPLE SUSPECTS
Under Siege

1. Calfas, J. (2017, March 22). Americans Have So Much Debt They're Taking It to The Grave. Retrieved from http://money.com/money/4709270/americans-die-in-debt/

2. Living Paycheck to Paycheck is a Way of Life for Majority of U.S. Workers, According to New CareerBuilder Survey. (2017, August 24). Retrieved from http://press.careerbuilder.com/2017-08-24-Living-Paycheck-to-Paycheck-is-a-Way-of-Life-for-Majority-of-U-S-Workers-According-to-New-CareerBuilder-Survey

3. Report on the Economic Well-Being of U.S. Households in 2017. (2018, May). Retrieved from https://www.federalreserve.gov/publications/2018-economic-well-being-of-us-households-in-2017-preface.htm

4. Maldonado, C. (2018, July 25). Price of College Increasing Almost 8 Times Faster Than Wages. Retrieved from http://www.forbes.com/sites/camilomaldonado/2018/07/24/price-of-college-increasing-almost-8-times-faster-than-wages/#28195bb466c1.

5. Steele, J. B., & Williams, L. (2018, August 10). Who got rich off the student debt crisis? Retrieved from http://www.revealnews.org/article/who-got-rich-off-the-student-debt-crisis/.

6. Wolff-Mann, E. (2018, August 08). Every Wells Fargo consumer scandal since 2015: A timeline. Retrieved from https://finance.yahoo.com/news/every-wells-fargo-consumer-scandal-since-2015-timeline-194946222.html

7. Dwyer, K. (2017, August 02). Timeline: How the Wells Fargo scandals unfolded. Retrieved from https://www.mcall.com/business/mc-biz-wells-fargo-timeline-20170802-story.html

Chapter 2: BORROW, LEST YOU BE FREE
Booby Trap

1. United States Gross Federal Debt to GDP. (n.d.). Retrieved from https://tradingeconomics.com/unitedstates/gover

<u>nment-debt-to-gdp</u>

2. Total Household Debt Rises for 17th Straight Quarter. (2018, November 16). Retrieved from <u>https://www.newyorkfed.org/newsevents/news/research/2018/rp181116</u>

3. Default. (n.d.). Retrieved from <u>https://fafsa.ed.gov/help/default.htm</u>

4. Gathergood, J. (2012, March 09). Debt and Depression: Causal Links and Social Norm Effects. Retrieved from <u>https://academic.oup.com/ej/article/122/563/1094/5079467</u>

5. Meltzer, Howard, Bebbington, Paul, Farrell, Michael, . . . Rachel. (2012, March 20). Relationship between personal debt and specific common mental disorders. Retrieved from <u>https://academic.oup.com/eurpub/article/23/1/108/464719</u>

6. Bethune, S. (2017, November 01). APA Stress in America™ Survey: US at 'Lowest Point We Can Remember;' Future of Nation Most Commonly Reported Source of Stress. Retrieved from <u>https://www.apa.org/news/press/releases/2017/11/lowest-point</u>

Chapter 4: STEP 2 – KNOW HOW MUCH YOU OWE
Don't Shoot Without a Target

1. Valdes, R. (2018, June 28). How Military Snipers Work. Retrieved from https://science.howstuffworks.com/sniper.htm

2. www.annualcreditreport.com.

3. Kiyosaki, R. (2017, November 28). Are You Stuck in the Holiday Rat Race? Retrieved from https://www.richdad.com/resources/rich-dad-financial-education-blog/november-2017/are-you-stuck-in-the-holiday-rat-race

4. Compound Interest Formula - Explained. (n.d.). Retrieved from https://www.thecalculatorsite.com/articles/finance/compound-interest-formula.php

5. Exponent Calculator. (n.d.). Retrieved from https://www.calculator.net/exponent-calculator.html

6. Loan Payoff Calculator. (n.d.). Retrieved from http://www.moneyunder30.com/loan-payoff-calculator.

7. Nova, A. (2018, September 21). Just 96 of 30,000 people who applied for public service loan forgiveness actually got it. Retrieved from https://www.cnbc.com/2018/09/21/the-education-

department-data-shows-how-rare-loan-forgiveness-is.html

8. Are you SMART? Goal Setting Lessons. (2019). Retrieved from https://www.whatihavelearnedteaching.com/product/are-you-smart-goal-setting-lessons/

Chapter 5: STEP 3 – BUDGET
Strategy and Tactics

1. Stanley, T. J., & Danko, W. D. (1996). *The Millionaire Next Door*. New York: Pocket.

Chapter 6: STEP 4 – STARTER EMERGENCY FUND
Build Your Walls – Protect Your City

1. Report on the Economic Well-Being of U.S. Households in 2017. (2018, May). Retrieved from https://www.federalreserve.gov/publications/2018-economic-well-being-of-us-households-in-2017-preface.htm

2. Huddleston, C. (2016, September 19). 69% of Americans Have Less Than $1,000 in Savings. Retrieved from https://www.gobankingrates.com/saving-money/savings-advice/data-americans-savings/

Chapter 7: STEP 4 – DECREASE EXPENSES + INCREASE INCOME
Two Sides of The Equation

1. Papadimitriou, O. (2018, March 17). How to Cancel a Credit Card Without Hurting Your Score. Retrieved from https://wallethub.com/edu/canceling-unused-credit-cards-and-credit-scores/25563/

2. Krome, C. (2018, November 09). Car Depreciation: How Much Value Will a New Car Lose? Retrieved from http://www.carfax.com/blog/car-depreciation.

3. Coffee Statistics. (n.d.). Retrieved from http://www.e-importz.com/coffee-statistics.php

4. Krstic, Z. (n.d.). These Are the Cheapest Grocery Stores in America. Retrieved from https://www.cookinglight.com/news/cheapest-grocery-stores

5. Uwa. (2016, May 15). The 3 P's to choosing the right career. Retrieved from http://www.uwasmif.com/smif-review/2016/5/15/the-3-ps-to-choosing-the-right-career

6. Home. (n.d.). Retrieved from https://www.focusgroup.com/

7. What is Affiliate Marketing About? (n.d.).
    Retrieved from
    https://successfulbusinessonline.org/affiliate-
    marketing

8. Shin, L. (2018, January 23). Work From Home
    2018: The Top 100 Companies For Remote Jobs.
    Retrieved from
    https://www.forbes.com/sites/laurashin/2018/01/1
    7/work-from-home-2018-the-top-100-companies-
    for-remote-jobs/#7f9c3d3276f0

Chapter 8: STEP 6 – ATTACK YOUR DEBT
Show No Mercy

1. Topic No. 201 The Collection Process. (2019, January
    28). Retrieved from https://www.irs.gov/taxtopics/tc201

2. Avalanches. (2009, October 09). Retrieved from
    https://www.nationalgeographic.com/environmen
    t/natural-
    disasters/avalanches/?user.testname=none.

3. Debt Snowball & Avalanche Payoff Calculator. (n.d.).
    Retrieved from
    https://tools.doughroller.net/debt-snowball-
    calculator/

4. Kettle, K. L., Trudel, R., Blanchard, S., & Haubl, G.
    (2016, August 09). Repayment Concentration and
    Consumer Motivation to Get Out of Debt. Retrieved

from
https://academic.oup.com/jcr/article-abstract/43/3/460/2200459?redirectedFrom=fulltext

5. Gal, D., & McShane, B. (2012, August 01). Can Small Victories Help Win the War? Evidence from Consumer Debt Management. Retrieved from https://journals.sagepub.com/doi/10.1509/jmr.11.0272

6. Nickerson, E. (2012, November 19). 4 Types of Loans You Can Refinance. Retrieved from https://www.themuse.com/advice/4-types-of-loans-you-can-refinance

7. National Health Service Corps. (2018, December 01). Retrieved from https://bhw.hrsa.gov/loansscholarships/nhsc

8. Nurse Corps. (n.d.). Retrieved from https://bhw.hrsa.gov/loansscholarships/nursecorps

9. Eligibility & Programs. (n.d.). Retrieved from https://www.lrp.nih.gov/eligibility-programs#ProgramsEligibilityLRPBenefitsTile

10. Costa, A. L., & Kallick, B. (2008). *Learning and leading with habits of mind: 16 essential characteristics for success.* Alexandria: Association for Supervision and Curriculum Development.

AUTHOR BIO

Leo Jean-Louis is a first-generation Haitian-American. At a very young age, he learned the value of being content with what you have and being resourceful. In middle school, he sold fun-sized candy bars he bought and resold to his peers for $0.25 each. He was able to save enough to buy himself his own full-sized basketball hoop! Over the years, Leo has spent the bulk of his time reading and learning about everything finance. After his post of paying off debt went viral on social media, he and his wife founded *Freedom Is A Choice Movement*, a business created to inspire everyone, everywhere to choose freedom from debt. His money tips and personal finance journey have been featured on Yahoo Finance, the Steve Harvey TV Show, the His & Her Money Show, MagnifyMoney, and Northwestern Mutual, just to name a few. Leo lives in Atlanta, Georgia with his beautiful wife, Faith, and they are expecting their first child this year.

PRODUCTS

FREEDOM METER

Product Description

Are you motivated to get out of debt? Tired of seeing your principal loan balance remain the same? Research shows that those who write down their goals _achieve significantly more_ than those who don't. Shop our new **FREEDOM METER** today for a simple visual to track your debt payoff goals and save thousands of dollars in interest payments! Remember, freedom is a choice and we're glad you're choosing to be free!

Price: $9.99

Visit **WWW.FREEDOMISACHOICEMVT.COM**

APPAREL

Check out our clothing line! This is the lifestyle component of our brand used for self-expression on your new journey to freedom! We are intentional about creating a line that not only serves as a style statement, but one that fosters conversation, engaging everyone who comes in contact with you. This is Fashion with a Purpose!

Visit **WWW.FREEDOMISACHOICEMVT.COM**

56881916R00176